Bitter Things

Narratives and Memories of Transnational Families

Archive Books

bi'bak

Table of Contents

Preface

When holiday time came, the children's parents came back to Turkey – mostly just the fathers. There were also children, whose fathers remained in Germany, but there were two children who were just like me: We would ask each other, "What did you get, what did they bring you," but we never asked "Are you not feeling alright" or something in that line.

Interview with **Tülay**, Munich 2017

I send smartphone chargers. He wants them. Not just a single one. "Send three or four," he says. He has a lot of wishes because I'm not there. I can't say "no" to his wishes. I just can't say: "One charger is enough, my son," for I'm living apart from him.

Interview with **Gülnar**, Istanbul 2017

In the 1960s and 1970s, it was the so-called guest workers in Germany who left their children behind in their native lands; today, it is predominantly migrant workers from Eastern Europe who leave their families behind to go in search of a living in economically better-off countries. Our first encounter with this phenomenon was unanticipated: through conversations with friends and acquaintances, we discovered that a great number of people in our immediate circle had been separated from their parents for some time during childhood. Initially, their parents had come to Germany without them to work. It quickly became clear to us that these are radical experiences, but rarely openly talked about. Presumably, owing to the fact that it was a taboo in families. As for the situation of many migrant workers today is concerned, the matter is simply disregarded. On numerous occasions, however, we have been encouraged, especially by those directly concerned, to grapple with the topic.

At the beginning of 2017, we began to take a more in-depth look at the life stories of transnational families with the series of events: *Zurückgelassen, Entwurzelt, Versteckt: Eltern- und Kinderschicksale der Arbeitsmigration* [Hidden, Uprooted, Left Behind: Parents' and Children's Fates of Labor Migration].

At bi'bak we have screened documentary and feature films on the topic, and invited authors to read from their works on the subject. The public's deep interest highly motivated us, and yet we realized that certain positions, perspectives, and questions in this series could not be rendered sufficiently visible. We thus decided to pursue our fieldwork and to give more space to the topic in an extensive project. The more we delve into our research, the clearer it becomes to us: Objects play a critical role in the relationships between transnational parents and their children. Despite geographical distance, parents strive to fulfill their parental role by supporting their children's material needs and educational careers. For the children, however, these objects or gifts are stuck in an ambivalent, tension-laden zone, hovering between memory, pain, hope, disappointment, and joy. While, for the parents, these objects reflect the wealth of the world in which they toil, in many cases they mean precious little to the children, whose deepest longing is none other than to be with their blood-parents.

This publication is part of the exhibition project *Bitter Things*, which we will be showing in Istanbul and Berlin in 2018, with an accompanying program of films, readings, and public discussions. We consciously decided in favour of a variety of diverse materials and text types: a mix of scientific and literary texts, song lyrics, excerpts from interviews, as well as images seeming most appropriate to adequately depict the topic's complexity. In doing so, it was vitally important for us to take into account the perspective of children and parents alike and, moreover, to look at the socio-political circumstances that led to and still lead to family divisions. While legal provisions on family reunion and reunification are currently being re-discussed in the context of refugee families, highlighting parallels with labour migration, especially in the retrospective about the so-called *Kofferkinder* [suitcase children], this publication hopes to expose the long-term scars that family separation can engender. It is thus all the more critical to stimulate discourse on the topic so that better action patterns can be developed through appropriate reappraisals.

Our special thanks to our cooperation partners *DOMiD* (Dokumentations-zentrum und Museum über die Migration in Deutschland e.V) for the use of their archive, and to *DEPO*, a space for culture, arts, and critical debate in Istanbul, who are ever-ready to make highly sensitive socio-political issues accessible to a general audience. We would also like to deeply thank our interviewees, as well as all those who agreed to talk with us with great candour about their often-painful memories. Many thanks also go to Ok-Hee Jeong and Bengü Kocatürk-Schuster, who repeatedly encouraged us about the project and wholeheartedly supported us throughout the process. We are glad to have found in *Archive* an ideal partner, not merely as publishers for the publication but also as an exhibition space, always ready with advice and support. We would also like to acknowledge our team that has supported us through this intense time as well as our families, who have constantly been at our side. Last but not least, our thanks also go to our patron, the Berlin Senate for Culture and Europe, without whom the project *Bitter Things* would not have seen the light of day.

By dint of this publication, we hope to furnish a differentiated overview of the work-related separation of transnational families, and thus to foster greater awareness about a reality of life that is the norm for many in our midst.

Malve Lippmann und Can Sungu
May 2018

Damned if They Go, Damned if They Don't

An Introduction by Maike Suhr

Furtive foreign lands you steal our young men
Bad magic! You bewitch us with money
You always separate mothers and children heartlessly

In his song *To ψωμί της ξενιτιάς* [The Bread of Foreign Lands], the Greek Rembetiko singer **Stelios Kazantzidis** curses foreign lands, which he characterises as "furtive" and "heartless," thereby expressing sad resignation. The hope for a better life by working abroad extracts a steep price to some extent: The separation and gradual alienation from home and family.

Family Separation during the Recruitment Agreements Period

This furtive foreign land, which **Kazantzidis** sings about at the time the lyrics were written in the 1970s, is the Federal Republic of Germany, the destination of numerous families not only from Greece, but also from Turkey, Italy, Yugoslavia, and other countries surrounding. One consequence of the German economic boom between 1955 and 1963 was that the federal government concluded a series of recruitment agreements for foreign workers in order to meet the high demands for industrial production. For a long-time it was assumed that workers migrating to Germany would merely stay a few years at most, and then return to their countries of origin. The term "guest workers" that took root in the 1960s, carries this notion of temporal limitation – a too short-lived assumption by decision-makers at that juncture, as we know today with retrospect. While most migrant workers may initially have had wanted to return to their native lands after a few years, it is only natural development that over time the concept of home becomes increasingly ambiguous and gradually overlaps with the new place of residence.

The basic idea of temporary work in the host country, however, did shape workers' daily lives; everything from consumer decisions to their living conditions to family reunions. In order to be able to save as much as possible for the return to their country of origin, migrants only bought the cheapest goods for themselves. The most inhumane lodgings were easier to tolerate in the knowledge that living there was only to be a stopgap measure. And as for their families, primarily the children, they were often left behind, initially with grandparents or with other relatives. After all, they would only be away for a year, maybe two, and the challenging working and living conditions in Germany would not allow them to provide childcare anyway.

And finally, was it not so that the children would have a better future should they as parents undertake this exhausting work in the first place. Getting used to both their new place of residence as well as a series of laws on residence permits and family reunions was eventually to lead to many families fetching their children, as **Gülcin Wilhelm** summarizes in her contribution *Generation Suitcase: The Children Left Behind.* As soon as the children arrived in Germany, the new home for the "guest workers" was consolidated and legitimized. Family reunification, however, often after many years of living apart was not always easy: the children had long become accustomed to their grandparents, aunts, or older siblings as their new caregivers. The accounts by **Stefano Polis** and **Ok-Hee Jeong** reveal how the trauma of separation from the parents is relived after being reunited with them.

For many years these accounts of separated families in the context of labour migration were not spoken about either by those directly affected, or by politicians: the matter never formed a part of general discourse. Meanwhile, it is widely known that those affected children, often referred to as *Kofferkinder* [suitcase children] or 'pendulum children' owing to their restless and rootless life between countries, have suffered greatly from the psychological consequences of leaving their homeland, and still suffer from them to this very day. Bonding difficulties and feelings of worthlessness are but some of the effects of the often unannounced disappearance by parents, as **Maria Papoulias** already noted in in her 1987 article *Suitcase Children – Mother - Child Separation As a Cause for Psychopathological Reactions among Migrant Worker Families.* While the theme of family separation in contemporary witness accounts, such as in the interviews and letters of the journalist **Georg Matzouranis** with Greek 'guest workers', is abundantly present, nowadays, with the growing visibility of its harmful consequences, the topic is subject to a widespread taboo. The children's finger pointing is often met with incomprehension by parents, who themselves had suffered from being separated and had to make sacrifices; they perceive their children's criticism as ingratitude to some extent.

Current Labour Migration and Family Separation

Although experiences by 'suitcase children' amply reveal the extent of the trauma caused by forced separation, the history of work-related broken families is currently being repeated by million-fold worldwide. In Germany, the nursing sector is currently dependent on workers from Poland, Ukraine, Romania, and other east European countries. These modern-day 'guest workers' are highly sought after, but often employed on an under the counter basis. Family reunification is not possible under these circumstances. No reliable data on the number of abandoned children in the post-Soviet countries is currently available, but in the Republic of Moldova alone, the Chişinău Children's Rights Information Centre estimates that there are 250,000 children (cf. Abé [2012] 2016). In Ukraine, the number even stretches into millions. Due to pressing demand in the care and nursing sectors in industrialized nations, labour migration has become progressively associated with women over recent years (cf. Morokvasic 2009). Work in the care sector is traditionally still perceived as a female confine. While migrant women help out domestically in German, British, Italian, or Spanish families, their own children back home have to get along in the absence of their mothers. Instead, neighbours, grandparents, or other relatives assume the parental role. A "global care chain" has emerged (Hochschild 2000), a chain formation of care relationships, whereby care work shifts from the migrant's own family to the employer family abroad, whereupon substitutes, in turn, must assume parental care and obligations in the home country.

Even Turkey, as an erstwhile country of widespread emigration, has itself become a host country over recent years. In many affluent families, it is now commonplace to employ domestic workers from the Philippines, Moldava, Ukraine, or Central Asia. **Ayşe Akalın**'s article *Doing Care, the Migrant Way: Transnational Mothering*, outlines the history of domestic migrant labour migration to Turkey from the 1950s to the present day. In particular, she addresses the challenges of transnational motherhood.

Transnational Families and Redefining Motherhood

The transnational family has long been a well-established family model in many regions of the world. Nina Glick-Schiller, Linda Basch, and Cristina Blanc-Szanton define transnational migrants as migrants who maintain a social network both in their country of origin and in their new place of residence (cf. Glick Schiller et al., 1992). The mobility of transnational mothers has lead to motherhood being redefined (Millman 2013). In transnational families care for the family is characterized by economic and material care; physical closeness, however, necessarily takes a secondary place given the circumstances. The discrepancy between the traditional and the new mother role, between expectations of the social environment in the country of origin and in the host country, are not straightforward for children and parents alike.

For all these individual destinies have one thing in common: the decision to leave their own children behind so as to make a living abroad is never taken recklessly. Rather, there are serious economic constraints under which migrant workers had to leave their countries of origin, and are still doing so nowadays. It is difficult to offset the impact of going abroad or staying in one place: while the financial hardship is markedly present, the emotional burden at first seems less serious. The psychological impact of having been left behind often only comes to surface years later. In most cases a tragic paradox holds true for the parents: Damned if they go, damned if they don't. **Halyna Kruk's** and **Liliana Corobca's** stories shed light on the pressured everyday life of transnational families from both sides – that of the child and of the parent. **Halyna Kruk's** *Ho Paura* describes a mother working in Italy attempting to communicate with her son in the Ukraine. Their Skype conversation is interrupted by technical disturbances and much remains unsaid. **Liliana Corobca's** *Kinderland* explores the perspective of twelve-year-old girl Cristina, who is taking care of her little siblings, while her mother and father work abroad and ensure their material well-being. The material aspect is repeatedly mentioned in the literary contributions in this volume; this manifests itself partly in the remittances sent back home, but also in the objects and gifts that to some extent take the place of a shared domestic relationship.

The Significance of Things and Objects for Transnational Families

Better bread and olive
in a humble house
Than thousands of goods
in bitter foreign lands

The singer **Kazantzidis** evokes the material temptations of foreign lands, which ultimately, as he states, cannot replace being near to one's home and family. In fact, the goods and gifts sent by labour migrants to their families home represent a critical aspect of the transnational family relationship, as **Ayşe Akalın** and **Janka Vogel** point out in their contributions. In the end, these offerings not only legitimize the parents' physical absence by providing the children with comfort, and, above all, are meant to furnish them with a better future; they also, however, symbolize the parent's economic success abroad. The financial and material support from family members working abroad is also a key contributor to gross national income for many low-output nations. In the Philippines, for example, the sending of gifts has even become a governmental program since 1987: Overseas Filipino workers could henceforth send duty-free packages, the *balikbayan boxes*, to relatives and friends back home.

And yet, gifts are not always without their problems on a personal level: "Mama doesn't send us any toys," laments protagonist Cristina in *Kinderland* by **Liliana Corobca**. Beautiful things would only arouse envy among other children, as did Cristina's new prom dress, which had burn marks by at the end of her evening at the ball. **Ok-Hee Jeong** also writes about her classmates' admiration and resentment of the gifts that her parents had sent her from West Germany in the 1970s. In **Stefano Polis'** story, however, gifts serve as an effective bait: with toys and sweets, the father, who has long since been a stranger to his children, tries – with success – to make their new overseas home palatable. In both the texts and narratives dating from the recruitment agreement period, as well as in relation to today's transnational family, time and time again it is stressed that nothing can replace parental closeness. And yet, transnational parents have to realize that children to some extent quickly get used to the gifts from abroad and soon start making demands. The letter to his father in a foreign country from a Turkish boy in the 1970s reads like an order list, in places.

The shift from the traditional mother role, simply reduced to the image of the material provider, is especially difficult for the mothers themselves. "For them you're the money-sender, the umpteen hundred-euro transfers, the voice on the phone that one asks to send this or that, you're the wish fulfilment machine," concludes the protagonist in the short story *Ho Paura*, wistfully. As soon as the family has become accustomed to the new standard of living, the mother's new-found role as provider from afar can no longer be reversed. And yet, as notes **Janka Vogel** in her contribution to *Transnational Romanian Families*, the material and financial support will enable the children to actually enjoy a better future and many of them would appreciate this as well.

In the course of research for the exhibition project of the same name *Bitter Things*, on the occasion of which this publication will appear, numerous interviews were conducted with children and parents alike, from several countries affected by migration. Here again, the question of the material aspect in transnational relations was pivotal. The interview excerpts and selected objects convey an impression of the individual life-stories, unveiling each family destiny, today as in the past.

Transnational Families in Popular Culture and in Current Discourse

The long-neglected topic of abandoned children in the context of labour migration is not only increasingly finding its way into science and literature – the motif of the transnational family is equally and constantly present in film or music in those countries concerned. Song lyrics thus constitute an indispensable supplement to the topic in this anthology. In addition to the fore-mentioned **Kazantzidis's** lament, both old and new songs from Turkey, from Yugoslavia, the Philippines, Ukraine and Romania are featured, ranging from pop music to teen stars to amateur YouTube videos in which people sing about being abandoned and the sense of absence, hopes, resignation, and foreign lands.

This book provides a regional framework, in particular by examining migration to Germany and to Turkey. The reason for choosing this geographic focus is that Germany and Turkey are interlinked through a long history of migration, and yet, both countries with their relatively stable labour markets have today become host countries for migrant workers from the world's economically disadvantaged regions. Some workers even come from the same countries of origin, such as Ukraine or the Republic of Moldova. In addition, transnational family relationships naturally exist in numerous other regions throughout the world as well. With a double temporal focus on both recruitment and labour migration, this volume seeks to provide a comprehensive overview of the phenomenon of abandoned children and transnational families, and thereby to create a greater public awareness of the resultant memories and aspirations, traumas and societal ramifications.

References

Abe, Nicola. [2012] 2016. Country without parents. In *Land ohne Eltern*. ed. Andrea Diefenbach. 70-73 Heidelberg, Berlin: Kehrer.

Millman, Heather L. 2013. "Mothering from Afar: Conceptualizing Transnational Motherhood," Totem: *The University of Western Ontario Journal of Anthropology*: Vol. 21: Iss. 1, Article 8.

Morokvasic, Mirjana. 2009. Migration, Gender, Empowerment. In: *Gender Mobil. Geschlecht und Migration in transnationalen Räumen,* ed. Helma Lutz. pp.29. Münster: Westfälisches Dampfboot,

Hochschild, Arlie 2000. Global Care Chains and Emotional Surplus Value. In *On the Edge: Living with Global Capitalism,* ed. Will Hutton and Anthony Giddens, 130-146. London: Jonathan Cape

Glick Schiller, Nina & Basch, Linda & Blanc-Szanton, Cristina 1992. Transnationalism: A New Analytic Framework for Understanding Migration. In: *Annals of the New York Academy of Sciences*. Issue 645, p. 1-24.

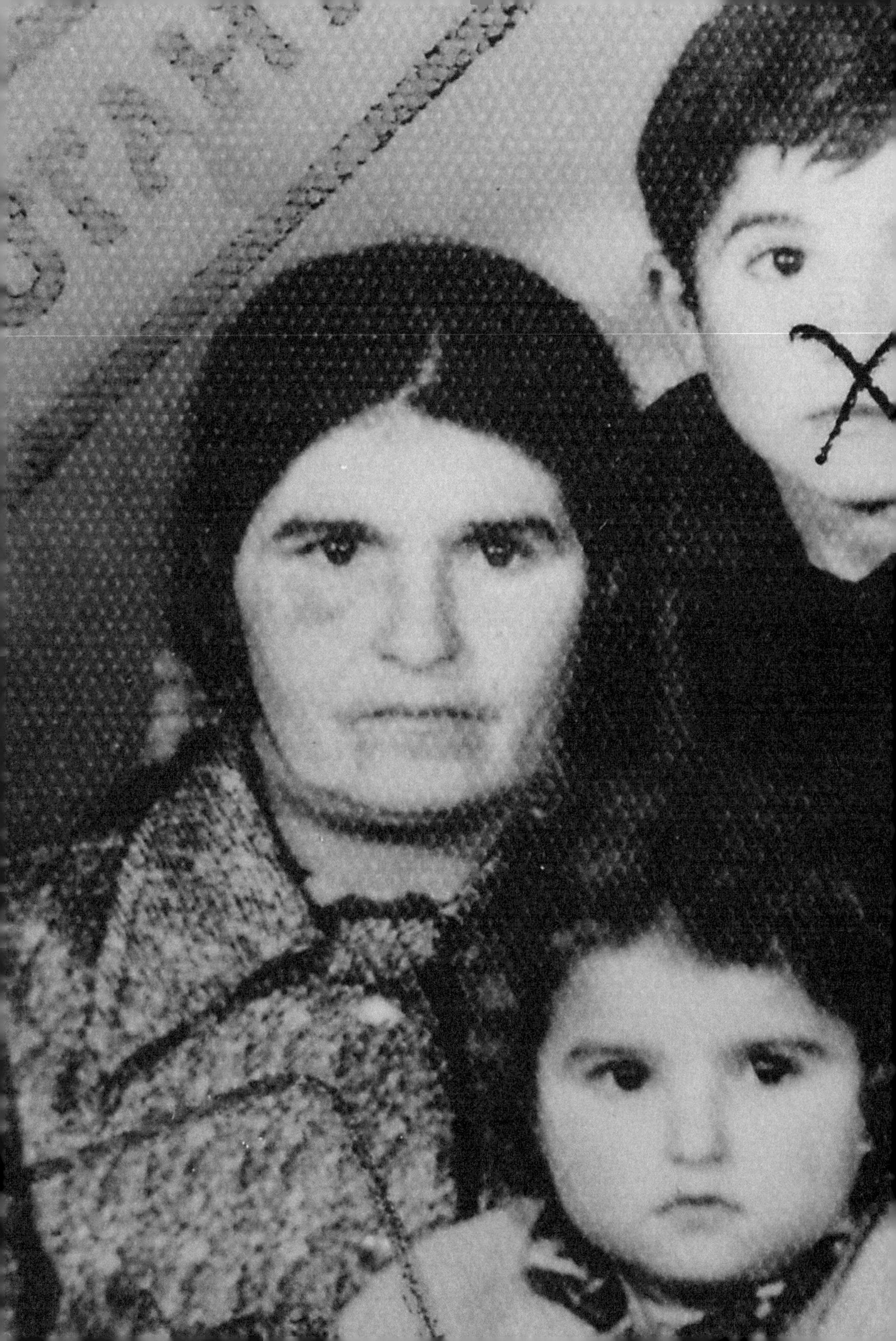

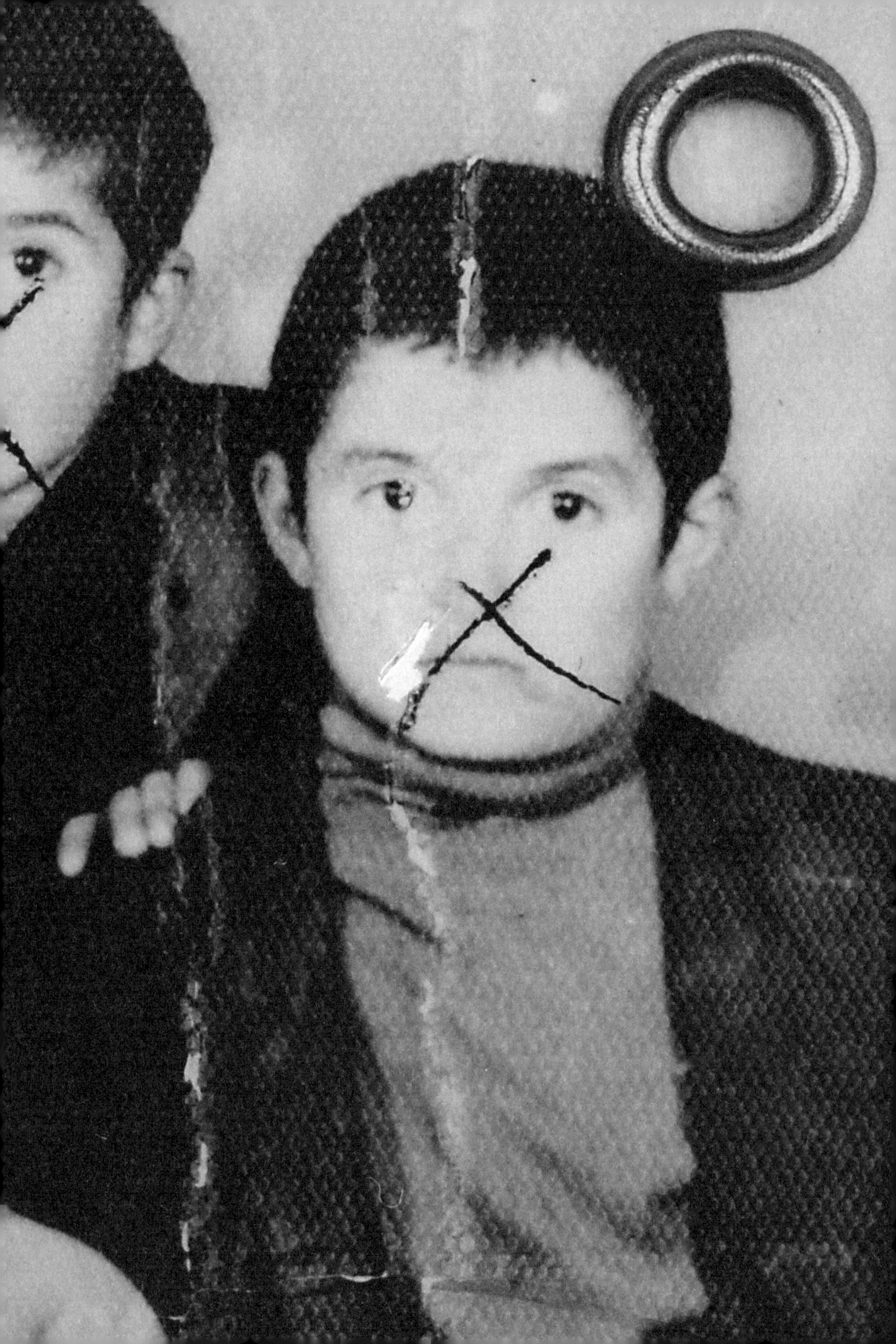

While many migrant workers from Turkey emigrated to Germany or
Austria in the 1960s and 1970s, Turkey itself has meanwhile become
a host country, notably following the collapse of the Soviet Union in the
early 1990s. Ayşe Akalın describes the historical and current situation
of migrant domestic workers in Turkey, the feminization of migration,
as well as the critical role of material gifts in transnational families.

Doing Care, the Migrant Way: Transnational Mothering

Ayşe Akalın

The Historical Context

In the Turkish context, there has been a manifest affinity between developments in urbanization and (professional) domestic help. In the early 20th Century, residential homes in the big cities were mainly two story buildings that rose in their own gardens. Domestic work was then procured by *live-in* so-called adopted daughters (Özbay 2007), which was a historically specific, liminal status between slavery and free labor in the realm of domestic work. These young women would have a common background in rural poverty and were taken in by affluent families based in the cities. As these families saw it in their mission to 'civilize' and/or Turkify these young women[1] while they were integrated in the modern urban settings, they would in return be expected to assist with house chroes fulltime. In exchange for being taught their manners and etiquette, these young women would be treated in the status of a Simmelian stranger (1971) by the household. In other words, they would be let into their employers' private household while, however, being denied to be treated as 'one of them.' The early Republican urbanization came to an end in the 1950's and 1960s when those houses with gardens got replaced by multi-story buildings (Duru 2006). It was in that same period that taking in 'adopted daughters' came to a demise while the rural-to-urban migration took off. Since the newly built residential flats were much smaller in size than their precedents, *live-in* domestic help became obsolete due to spatial and financial constraints. Professional domestic work instead was taken over by the women of the internal migrants who not only needed jobs to survive the harsh economic conditions of the new city life but were also deemed as unskilled to be employed in any other field than domestic work. Contrary to the adopted daughters of the previous era, these women of the new urban poor lived in their own homes with their families. Therefore, they could only work as *live-out* workers, which suited the new demand coming from the new life style of the urban middle class families (Kalaycıoğlu and Rittersberger-Tılıç 2000).

The third period to the urbanization-domestic work linkage came in the late 1990's. In the realm of urbanization, this was the time of suburbanization, when many of the apartment buildings were turned into high rise 'residences' or gated communities of big houses with gardens (Genis 2007, Kurtulus 2005).

Furthermore, in such residential compounds lived families of full time working parents who now created a new demand for full-time *live-in* domestic workers who would take over many of the traditional responsibilities of either child care or housework or both (Akalın 2008). This demand for a novel form of professional domestic help was met via mechanisms of globalization that pushed new

---

1 Many of them were taken in from non-Muslim families (Özbay 2012).

migration waves into Turkey. More specifically, 1990s was also the period of postsocialism, when the Iron Curtain had fallen down, leaving all the former Soviet and socialist republics and their citizens abruptly alone with their own fate. While the mobility of the Soviet citizens within and out of the union was something that was once strictly controlled by the government, for millions of citizens of these former socialist republics, out-mobility became an indispensable form of survival in the immediate aftermath of postsocialism.

Yet a third development of the 1990s was Turkey's transition from once being a source of migration into one that received migration. Its geographic location that placed it not only in short proximity to various postsocialist countries but also between Europe and Asia and Africa has rapidly turned Turkey into a place where migration flows with various goals, and political statuses, passed through (İçduygu 2004, 2006).

Thus out of the combination of all these factors, in Turkey the new practice of employing migrant women as *live-in* domestic workers emerged. While the first migrant domestics of the 1990's came from countries to the west of Turkey, from places such as Moldova, Ukraine and Bulgaria, the increasing demand for this novel mode of domestic services created new pull mechanisms from places to the east of Turkey, such as Georgia, Turkmenistan, Uzbekistan and Kyrgyzstan. Irrespective of where they come from, migrant domestics have been demanded for three main tasks; as caregivers to children, caregivers to the elderly and as full time maids or house-keepers in the houses of gated communities or 'residence' flats.

Doing Care from a Distance: From 'Feminization of Migration' to 'Transnational Mothering'

There is perhaps one other common trait that characterizes most, if not all, migrant domestics who work in Turkey, and that is their solo travels to Turkey. The migrant domestics in Turkey is a good example to the "feminization of migration". This is a concept introduced by Stephen Castles in his seminal text *The Age of Migration*, to point out the novel developments that are likely to become the future trends in international migration (1998). In a nutshell, the concept refers to the increase in the number of women pursuing migration whether as refugees or as laborers. In doing so, these women become the primary or sole breadwinners of their families at home, which is contrary to early forms of gendered migration when women would travel as part of family unification or while accompanying their spouses. To give an idea about this increase, the Global Commission on International Migration have declared that in the early 2000s, half of the international migrants were women (GCIM Report 2005), which is unprecedented.

As Parreñas has once argued, immigration policies have a strong influence on family dynamics (2005a). Consequently, a significant outcome of the feminization of migration is another related concept of the migration literature, "transnational motherhood". Succinctly, this concept aims to recount what happens to the care duties of mothers when they leave home to become migrants. Unlike other kinds of responsibilities, motherhood is a contract that does not cease, or even dwindle, even in the case of physical separation between the mother and her children. Yet, even on the mother-child bond, which is arguably the strongest bond of all, the physical separation does place a heavy burden and prompts it to transform itself into new forms so that it can continue flourishing even in these physically constraining circumstances. In other words, women's migration ultimately turns into a challenge on mothering that tests not its durability perhaps, but its flexibility and resilience that then leads to creating novel forms of perseverance to divert the strains on it caused by the distances separating its subjects.

Ostensibly transnational mothering may appear at first sight as the opposite of "intensive mothering", a concept coined by Sharon Hays to describe "a gendered model that advises mothers to expend a tremendous amount of time, energy, and money in raising their children" (1998, x). Yet, in reality, transnational mothering becomes nothing other than "intensive mothering at a distance" (Madianou 2012, Madianou and Miller 2011) though of course pursued in its particular ways, such as in the mode of "double living" (Boccagni, 266) or "double presence" (Carling et al. 2012). Transnational mothering requires mothers to simultaneously follow her employer's directives at work and the developments that occur in her absence at her own home, or in other words have their bodies in one place and their soul in the other.

Feminization of migration and transnational mothering are therefore concepts embedded in each other. Formulated by Mirca Madianou as "accentuated ambivalence" (2012), the two concepts inextricably constitute the two faces of women's migration. Put differently, when a woman in the identity of motherhood faces the prospect of migration, she simultaneously faces a challenge that will test her love towards her children no matter which option she pursues. If she chooses to go and seek work abroad, she will not only have to accept living a period of her life away from her children, but may also be accused of being a bad mother for doing so, as well (Keough 2015). Yet, if she does not take on migration, then her family is likely to suffer from the deprecating economic and/or political conditions that they are already in, which will not only impact herself but more importantly her own children. Hence in the case of "accentuated ambivalence", the moral and ethical questions of motherhood become "what exactly does it mean to love your children? If the well-being of one's children is deemed a primary responsibility of mothering, how does one take good care of them in the best way possible when she is unable to provide for them economically *and* emotionally at the same time?" In other words, as ostensible as it may appear, transnational mothering is always the result of a choice made for the well-being of children, which then coagulates into the formulation of its own particular methods to carry out that goal. Whatever form it takes, the end result unavoidably presents a challenge on the emotional bond between the children and the mothers.

Yet, mothers then seek to overcome this challenge by converting affective ties into material and financial means. The latter distinction is critical. Since its initial formulation by Hondagneu- Sotelo (1997), transnational mothering has been the topic of numerous research and studies. In a nutshell, these studies take an empirical look at how individual cases deal with the tension between the interpellation of women into motherhood, and the ineludible mechanisms of flexible copings that somehow try to resist and remold the physical separation between the mothers and the children. While the will to support a better future for the children is the ultimate aim in the initiation of the feminization of migration, providing for the financial needs of the children is hardly sufficient when it comes to mothering. The ultimate challenge facing mother-migrants is the feeling of abandonment that they are likely to cause on their children. Therefore, as 'money can't buy love', it becomes necessary to find other means that would convert the non-material forms of love also into tangible forms. This is so that both two sides can still share a sense that they are connected, despite all the odds and pursue nonetheless a form of "care at a distance" (Leifsen and Tymczuk 2012, 219).

The Material and Informational Compensations of Transnational Mothering

Of these coping mechanisms that aim to convert the emotional bond between the mother and the child in more tangible forms, two are recurrently mentioned in the literature (Asuncion and Fresnoza-Flot 2009). That's mainly because they yield mechanisms more efficacious in overcoming the physicality of the separation than most others. The first one of these is "gift giving". In the physical absence of their own guardianship, the mothers opt to compensate for the time lost to being apart by buying and sending home material objects as an alternative means for showing their love. According to Fresnoza-Flot, these gift givings "express love, symbolize gratitude, upward social mobility, [and] affirm their place in family" (258). The famous *balikbayan box*, a box filled with goodies that Filipinas send home about twice a year for example, is an epitome of this compulsion to transfigure their emotional bonds toward their family members into tangible objects (259). In other words, these gifts not only work to turn the time spent apart into palpable forms but to also convey the message that there is no turning back for that family to the time before the migration. The objects signify that the sacrifices made by all the family members were made to add up to some form of improvement for everyone involved.

Yet, gift giving is not necessarily a standard practice pursued in the same way by all migrant mothers. Fresnoza-Flot states that when mothers are away in undocumented status they rather resort to monetary gifts than objects (2009). The status of the mothers becomes important in these kind of matters because it restricts the mothers' will to pay visits home on a regular basis, a point raised also by Leifsen and Tymczuk when they talk about the need to shift our attention to the political circumstances that transnational families "do" transnational relatedness under (2012, 221). Fresnoza-Flot argues that undocumented mothers opt for monetary gift giving because they feel the long periods of time they have spent away from home have caused them to lose touch with the likes and dislikes of their children. The second primary mechanism of coping with pursing lives apart is the intensive use of technology so as to somehow be "(re)connected." Endeavors of being connected despite the distance has always been an affective part of the migration experience. Previously this need would be fulfilled with what we would now deem as the dated means of technology, such as letters, phone calls, tapes and videos. Ultimately, these means of communication would serve the function of being the "bridges of constant communication" (Parreñas 2001, 142).

In today's world, on the other hand, that need is satisfied by international communication technologies, or ICTs (Leifsen and Tymczuk 2012, 220). Yet as it would be expected, ICTs facilitate the maintenance of an unprecedented form of bonding among migrant family members that the technological means of previous periods would not allow for. In the words of Carling et al., they "confirm" the relations between the migrant parents and their children despite the time spent apart (2012, 203). Scholars therefore give new names to these novel forms of bonding, such as "technological management of family relations" (Parreñas 2001a, Parreñas 2001b), or "virtual intimacies" (Wilding 2006). While of course the regular use of technology in such circumstances is contingent on a number of factors, such as whether the technological infrastructure where children are based is sufficient for this or not, the possibility of accessing cheap devices has nonetheless made ICTs a common part of the current transnational family experience.

What's more, with the increasing popularization of these technological means, the possibilities go beyond mere communication. They also facilitate a form of monitoring on the part of the mother/parents over the daily lives of their children. Depending on their work circumstances, they may have the time to follow the daily routine of the children even on an hourly basis, keeping an eye on their diet, their homework and other similar daily activities. Such developments have certainly had consequences for the way migrant women practice transnational mothering. While these technological developments may help to ease their feelings of guilt for being away from their children, they also add onto their responsibilities of 'being here and being there' at the same time. In other words, ICTs have been the ultimate facilitator in turning transnational mothering into "intensive mothering at a distance" (Madianou 2012).

The 'Other' Mothers

Yet, of course, these remedies can only compensate for the physical absence of mothers to an extent. We have to remember that mothering is not only about the emotional support of the children. The children will of course also need to be tended for physically. When mothers migrate, there will always have to be other designated-mother(s)-on-site. These usually are some close relatives, sisters or mothers, from either side of the parents. In the migration literature, this is what's known as the "global care chain" (Hochschild 2000, Hochschild and Ehrenreich 2004). The latter points out the activation of a series of transnational relations that in some cases even stretch across the global North/ South divide leading to an unintended extension of relations between families of very different locations of the global capitalism. As the families of the North create a demand for labor power in feminized forms of work, this stirs first a supply out of the global South, which then leads to a care deficit in the supplying families. The deficit is then compensated for by the other women in the family. Also referred to as "International Division of Reproductive Labor" (Parreñas 2000), or "the transnational fostering triangle" (Akesson et. al. 2012), or "second mothers" (Menjivar 2012, 314), women's migration triggers a domino effect in the provision of physical care for the children. In fact, some scholars argue that when the care of the children is handed over to these "other-mothers", the relationship between them and the children transcends one that is based on the mere maintenance of the children's physical care. In some cases, the children's emotional dependence on their immediate biological relatives may in fact wane in time, turning the actual mothers into the "other mothers" of their own children (Bloch 2017).

Doing Transnational Mothering in Turkey

A very interesting aspect of the feminization of migration literature is its wide applicability to the empirical data collected from very different places around the world. In other words, much of what has been reiterated here from the literature so far is in fact a summary of what happens to the migrant domestics in Turkey (and elsewhere), as well. For many of them, the choice to come to Turkey has

been closely related with their responsibility of considering the future and the well-being of their children. In the immediate period following post-socialism, not only was there cash shortage caused by a scarcity in job opportunities but with the collapse of the public services of the former socialist states, basic needs such as education and health services could only be attained in exchange for cash. Therefore, there was almost an indubitable need to go seek work elsewhere and send money home to pay off the debts and attain the immediate needs of the family members, most often the children.

Yet, some of my interviewees would reveal their sense that their own feminization of migration was a consequence of their husbands' reluctance to make similar kinds sacrifices as theirs. While it was true that job opportunities were scarce in their own countries for both genders, there were opportunities for men elsewhere, such as the construction work sector in Russia. Pursuing this opportunity would, as those women claimed, save their families from having to suffer through the traumatic repercussions of having the mothers be gone for long periods of time. How each family makes the decision of which family member to send away as its primary bread winner from migration is a complicated topic that requires further scrutiny, of course. However, it's worth pointing out here the difference in the ways domestic work and construction labor are organized. In Turkey, many employer families often tend to financially and symbolically invest in a domestic worker whose services they arepleased with. So they may be willing to give her extra compensations that includes paying their worker's travel expenses to home and back, sending gifts to her children, or letting her children come stay with them for a while in the summer. Construction work, on the other hand, can become more precarious in more standard ways. Workers may just not get paid their regular salaries, or may get laid off abruptly. In other words, the feminization of migration holds a potential to turn into long term work. The husbands' precarious labor in other low paying sectors, however, often times does not offer this prospect. Therefore, in opting to migrate, many migrant women employed in Turkey would not make their decision on the basis of available job opportunities just in the short run but in the consideration for the possibility to extend their terms in Turkey, as well. The latter would mean a regular income for the whole family and the chance to financially take care of the kids at home for an extended period. Therefore, when the assessment was made not on the basis of which parent would be available to go away, but on the viability of opportunities for each parent, many families would be likely to opt for the mother to take the journey, mainly for the long term benefits and perks that she could possibly bring to the whole family.

Transnational Fathers

Having focused on transnational mothering so far, it's also worth comparing it with what happens to fathering in migration. Perhaps the starting point for this is a reminder that there is not an "intensive" equivalent version to fathering (Pribilsky 2012). In other words, different from mothering that is deemed bound to re-adjust itself into the new circumstances even when distances keep its actors apart (Parreñas 2001b, 2005a), fathering is not expected to yield a similar kind of acclimation. The difference here lies in the fact that while fathers' physical absence, too, is likely to cause an emotional dis-placement for the children, it will not however cause alterations into care routine of the children. Ultimately, when fathers go away for work, they continue being imagined as following their gender roles and therefore not technically deemed as "abandoning" their children (Parreñas 2008, Dreby 2006). In such circumstances, mothers assume the role of both parents that is deemed as too different from the daily routine, had the father not be gone.

As a matter of fact, sometimes being the migrant parent may make fathers cherish and fulfill their fathering responsibilities even more. This becomes more apparent when migrant fathers' behavior is com-pared with those who have stayed with their children in the absence of their wives. Migrant fathers may relatively do far more child related work and get more interested in the developments around their children's lives because their income and therefore their financial contribu-tions to their families allow for their masculinity to be left intact and secure. "Absentee fathers" as Parreñas (2005a) has called them, or those fathers who have stayed at home with the children while their wives have become migrants, on the other hand, become present but not available around them by doing more "manly" yet less fatherly things like drinking just to avoid domestic work (Gamburd 2000). In other words, a reversal in gender roles is likely to be handled much more smoothly when the mother is the physical guardian of the children, but not so much when that work is left to the father.

A Last Note

As a last note, I want to add in my two penny worth to this intricate topic. In understanding the surging importance of feminization of migration, I think it is important to see the efforts that women perform in 'being here and there' at the same time not simply as endeavors to do care or to keep the family life going, but as mechanisms that valorize women's labor in unprecedented ways, as well. First of all, the fact that due to the feminization of migration, the children are not within the immediate reach of the mothers gives an assurance for the employers that their worker's professional performance will not be obstructed by her children's daily needs (Akalın 2015, Briggs 2017). Yet, their ceaseless devotion to the life at home is a further affirmation that their worker will take their job seriously in pleasing her employers and will work hard to turn her services into a long time commitment for them. In other words, as they step out of their own cocoons and take along their gendered ways of doing labor, women simultaneously prompt the prevalence of new mechanisms in the valorization of labor and a subsequent demand for that labor.

References

Akalın, Ayşe. 2008. "Die dort oben – die da unten: Die Beschäftigung von Migrantinnen als Haushaltsbedienstete in Istanbuler gated communitys." In *Facetten internationaler Migration in die Türkei: Gesellschaftliche Rahmenbedingungen und persönliche Lebenswelten*, edited by Barbara Pusch and Toman Wilkoszewski, Würzburg: Ergon.

Akalın, Ayşe. 2015. "Motherhood as the Value of Labour." In *Australian Feminist Studies 30*, no.83: 65-81

Akesson, Lisa, Jørgen Carling, and Heike Drobohm. 2012. "Mobility, Moralities and Motherhood: Navigating the Contingencies of Cape Verdean Lives." In *Journal of Ethnic and Migration Studies 38*, no. 2: 237-260.

Bloch, Alexia. 2017. "Other Mothers, Migration, and a Transnational Nurturing Nexus." In *Signs: Journal of Women in Culture and Society 43*, no. 1: 53-75.

Boccagni, Paolo. 2012. "Practising Motherhood at a Distance: Retention and Loss in Ecuadorian Transnational Families." In *Journal of Ethnic and Migration Studies 38*, no. 2: 261-277.

Briggs, Laura. 2017. *How All Politics Became Reproductive Politics: From Welfare Reform to Foreclousure to Trump.* Oakland: University of California Press.

Carling, Jørgen, Cecilia Menjivar and Leah Schmalzbauer. 2012. "Central Themes in the Study of Transnational Parenthood." In *Journal of Ethnic and Migration Studies 38*, no. 2: 191-217.

Castles, Stephen, and Mark J. Miller. 1998. *The Age of Migration.* New York: The Guilford Press.

Dreby, Joanna. 2006. "Honor and Virtue: Mexican Parenting in the Transnational Context". *In Gender and Society 20*, no.1: 32-59.

Duru, Asli. 2006. *Apartmentalization and Middle Classes: Urban Socio-Spatial Change in the Period 1950-1970s.* Master's thesis, The Ataturk Institute for Modern Turkish History, Bogazici University.

Geniş, Şerife. 2007. "Producing Elite Localities: The Rise of Gated Communities in İstanbul." In *Urban Studies 44*, no. 4: 771-798.

Fresnoza-Flot, Asuncion. 2009. "Migration Status and Transnational Mothering: the Case of Filipino Migrants in France." In *Global Networks 9*, no. 2: 252–270.

Gamburd, Michele Ruth. 2000. *The Kitchen Spoon's Handle: Transnationalism and Sri Lanka's Migrant Housemaids.* Ithaca: Cornell University Press.

Hays, Sharon. 1998. *The Cultural Contradictions of Motherhood.* New Hamshire: New York.

Hochschild, Arlie Russel. 2000. "Global Care Chains and

Emotional Surplus Value." In *On the Edge: Living with Global Capitalism*, edited by Will Hutton and Anthony Giddens. London: Jonathan Cape: 130-146.

Hochschild, Arlie Russel, and Barbara Ehrenreich. 2004. *Global Woman: Nannies, Maids, and Sex Workers in the New Economy*. London: Granta.

Hondagneu-Sotelo, Pierrette, and Ernestine Avila. 1997. "I'm Here, but I'm There: The Meanings of Latina Transnational Motherhood". In *Gender and Society 11*, no. 5: 548-571.

İçduygu, Ahmet. 2004. "Demographic Mobility and Turkey: Migration Experiences and Government Responses." In *Mediterranean Quarterly 15*, no.4: 88-99.

İçduygu, Ahmet. 2006. "Labour Dimensions of Irregular Migration." In *Research Report CARIM- RR 05*: http://cadmus.eui.eu/bitstream/handle/1814/6266/CARIM-RR2006_05.pdf?sequence=1

Kalaycıoğlu, Sibel, and Helga Rittersberger-Tılıç. 2000. *Evlerimizdeki Gündelikçi Kadınlar*. Ankara: Su Yayınları.

Keough, Leyla J. 2015. *Worker-Mothers on the Margins of Europe: Gender and Migration between Moldova and Istanbul*. Bloomington: Indiana University Press.

Kurtuluş, Hatice. 2005. "İstanbul'da Kapalı Yerleşmeler: Beykoz Konakları Örneği İstanbul'da Kentsel Ayrışma," In *İstanbul'da Kentsel Ayrışma*, edited by Hatice Kurtuluş. İstanbul: Bağlam: 161-186.

Leifsen, Esben, and Alexander Tymczuk. 2012. "Care at a Distance: Ukrainian and Ecuadorian Transnational Parenthood from Spain" In *Journal of Ethnic and Migration Studies 38*, no. 2: 219-236.

Madianou, Mirca. 2012. "Migration and the Accentuated Ambivalence of Motherhood: the Role of ICTs in Filipino Transnational Families". In *Global Networks 12*, no. 3: 277-295.

Madianou, Mirca, and Daniel Miller. 2011. "Mobile Phone Parenting: Reconfiguring Relationships between Filipina Migrant Mothers and Their Left-Behind Children." In *New Media & Society 13*, no.3: 457-470.

Menjivar, Cecilia. 2012. "Transnational Parenting and Immigration Law: Central Americans in the United States." In *Journal of Ethnic and Migration Studies 38*, no. 2: 301-322.

Report of the Global Commision on International Migration (GCIM). 2005. *Migration in an Interconnected World: New Directions for Action*. Switzerland: SRO-Kundig. Online availabe here: https://www.iom.int/global-commission-international-migration

Özbay, Ferhunde. 2007. *Kölelikten Evlatlıga: Osmanlı İmparatorlugunda Kölecilik ve Dönüsümü*. Presentation at the 'L'Esclavage africain sous l'Empire ottoman et les adoptions d'enfants d'esclaves' Conference, Paris, March 30.

Özbay, Ferhunde. 2012. "Türkiye'de Ev Emeginin Dönüsümü: Göç Ettirilen Kölelerden Kaçak Göçmen İşçilere." In *Geçmişten Günümüze Türkiye'de Kadın Emegi*, edited by Ahmet Makal and Gülay Toksöz, Ankara: Ankara Üniversitesi Yayınevi:116– 159.

Simmel, Georg. 1971. "The Stranger". In *Georg Simmel on Individuality and Social Forms*. Chicago: The University of Chicago Press.

Parreñas, Rhacel Salazar. 2000. "Migrant Filipina Domestic Workers and the International Division of Reproductive Labor." In *Gender and Society 14*, no. 4 : 560-580.

Parreñas, Rhacel Salazar. 2001a. "Mothering from a Distance: Emotions, Gender, and Intergenerational Relations in Filipino Transnational Families." In *Feminist Studies 27*, no. 2: 361–90.

Parreñas, Rhacel Salazar. 2001b. *Servants of Globalization: Women, Migration and Domestic Work*. Stanford, CA: Stanford University Press.

Parreñas, Rhacel Salazar. 2005a. *Children of Global Migration: Transnational Families and Gendered Woes*. Stanford, CA: Stanford University Press.

Parreñas, Rhacel Salazar. 2005b. "Long Distance Intimacy: Class, Genderand Intergenerational Relations between Mothers and Children in Filipino Transnational Families." In *Global Networks 5*: 317-333.

Parreñas, Rhacel Salazar. 2008. "Transnational Fathering: Gendered Conflicts, Distant Disciplining and Emotional Gaps." In *Journal of Ethnic and Migration Studies 34*, no.7: 1057-72.

Pribilsky, Jason. 2012. "Consumption Dilemmas: Tracking Masculinity, Money and Transnational Fatherhood Between the Ecuadorian Andes and New York City." In *Journal of Ethnic and Migration Studies 38*, no. 2: 323-343.

Wilding, Raelene. 2006. "Virtual Intimacies? Families Communicating across Transnational Contexts." In *Global Networks 6*, no.2: 125-42.

With more than 90,000 children whose parents are currently working abroad, the example of Romania renders particularly evident the relevance of the transnational family. With her analysis of how labor migration has impacted the individual, family, and social dimension, the the social worker and researcher in Romanian studies Janka Vogel explores the phenomenon of today's transnational Romanian family.

Transnational Romanian Families

Janka Vogel

Isn't it better,
if you'd stay in your country,
where you were born,
what gave you free education, what
dressed you and made you a human?
What's wrong with you, man?
Cărtărescu (2014)

Silviu's last days in prison. A movie scene located somewhere in southern Romania. Nowadays - even if the prison looks like a communist one. Silviu is a teenager who gets visited by his little brother. A foreign looking woman is waiting for him at the car. The little brother was raised by Silviu, so he gets nervous when he tells him about their mothers' plans. She, the woman with the car, came back from Italy just some days ago. And she will leave again, taking Silvius brother with her. Finally she talks to Silviu herself and tries to explain her decision, still hesitating to tell the full truth about her new Italian life. Is there a new family, too? A new man in her life? The woman visiting her son in jail embodies dramatically the effort for an identity, for a family, for doing good. Success and failure at the same time. She is here, but she is there, too.

The Romanian film *If I Want To Whistle, I Whistle* (Șerban 2010) is just one example for the popularity of the topic of Romanian children left behind in Romanian popular culture and daily life. Another one would be the documentary *Home Alone. A Romanian Tragedy* (Manu 2010) about the suicides of Nicolae and

Răzvan from eastern Romania, whose mothers worked in Italy as well. In 2015 the Romanian band Voltaj participated at the European Song Contest with the song *All Over Again*, telling the story of a boy whose parents are working in Austria. "More than 3 million Romanians are working abroad, trying to make a better life for their children," informs the video clip in the end. "Unfortunately, the children are left behind" (Voltaj 2015).

The phenomenon of separated families due to working migration is not only a Romanian problem. Transnational families exist all over the world. The heartbreaking documentary *Mama illegal* (Moschitz 2011) portaits transnational families between Moldova and Italy. Just some kilometers from the homes of these families at the same time the German photographer Andrea Diefenbach undertook her sensitive project *Land without Parents* (Diefenbach 2013). In the Ukraine you can find similar stories, as the anthology *Skype Mama* shows, portraying the efforts of the separated mothers and children to keep up communication (Brunner et al. 2013).

Children left back home with their older brothers and sisters, grandmothers, aunts and uncles or neighbors are one aspect of transnational families. Maybe it's the most striking one. However, it is the most mediatized one. In most of the cases the story goes like this: In need of (better payed) jobs people have to leave their home countries. Their left behind children are the victims of this unchangeable situation. But at least they can be thankful, because their parents are doing all this only for their (better) future. But is this the whole truth about it? In this article I will share some additional and critical thoughts about transnational families in and from Romania.

On Migration and Transnationality

Migration is as old as mankind itself. In search of better living conditions, employment, education or for other personal or social reasons people are leaving the places where they were born. Migration is strongly related to political and economic circumstances as well. From my point of view migration is always political in the sense that the decision to migrate is always a political one. People say 'yes' or 'no' to their home societies, and are more or less forced to do so.

There are quite a lot of different forms of migration. Scholars of migration studies distinguish between short and long term migration, the different reasons for migration (search for asylum, work, family reunification, studying, ...), the qualification of the migrants (high professionals vs. low educated) or the countries involved in the migrational process (emigration, immigration, transmigration, EU mobility, ...).

The notion of 'transnational migration' is a relatively new one. Since the 1990's scholars from the US[1] and later on from different regions in Europe[2] observed that migrants did not simply emigrate from their home country and immigrate into a new county. Migrant workers started to make their lives in both states – the one of origin and the one of destination.

The postmodern and globalized world of the late 20th and the early 21st century provoked transnational migration flows in two main ways.

First global capitalism and the spreading of the neoliberal order from the western hemisphere all over the world caused a worldwide growing impoverishment. Global warming, civil wars, land grabbing, corruption, agreements on so called free trade and waste of resources are reasons for this. The mass of homeless, landless and unemployed people is growing. The strongest of them try to search for (better paid) jobs in other regions. Migration flows at large go from the East to the West and from the South to the North.

The second aspect which caused an increase in transnational migration movements are nowadays' better infrastructural conditions for migration. Internet, television, Skype, mobile phones, but also (sometimes very cheap) transportation, money sending and delivery services do make life between two countries easier. Political agreements and

---

1 As for instance Glick Schiller, Nina; Basch, Linda; Szanton Blanc, Cristina. 1997. From Immigrant to Transmigrant: Theorizing Transnational Migration. In: *Ludger Pries (Ed.): Transnationale Migration 12*, 1st ed. Nomos Verlagsgesellschaft (Soziale Welt).

2 The most popular German scholars are Ludger Pries and Thomas Faist; see for instance Pries, Ludger (Ed.) 1997. In *Transnationale Migration*, 1st ed. Nomos Verlagsgesellschaft (Soziale Welt) and Faist, Thomas; Fauser, Margit; Kivisto, Peter (Ed.) 2011. The Migration-Development Nexus. Transnational Perspectives: palagrave; macmillan.

visa liberalizations are very important factors as well.

But all these factors – the negative and the positive ones – do exist to varying extents. Transnational migration in one region is not directly comparable with transnational migration in another region. Distance, working conditions, languages, currency, educational systems, ages of the family members, traditions, corruption rates and many other factors make every story of transnational migration more or less unique.

Romania and its transnational Migrants

The transnationalization of the Romanian working class started right after the fall of the iron curtain in 1990. The system transition from communism to liberal market economy and democracy made Romania struggle a lot. Politics were characterized by the former communist, later on so called social-democratic elites. In the first years after 1990 almost 4 Million jobs were lost, when factories were closed down. Their productivity could not cope with the rules of the globalized world. The European and international market was not waiting for Romanian products.

So many of the former urban citizens moved back to the countryside so they could feed their children with subsistence agriculture. Additionally more and more Romanians searched for jobs abroad. The Romanian sociologist Dumitru Sandu points out, that transnational migration became a life strategy (Sandu 2000). Before visa liberalizations in 2002 many Romanian citizens lived and worked illegally in foreign countries such as Israel, Turkey and Hungary. Since the mid 1990s Spain and Italy became important destination countries, mostly because of their expansion of the agricultural sector where low skilled harvest workers are needed. Great Britain, France and Germany are significant countries of destination, too.

Already 20 years ago Romania started to react on the exodus of its citizens. First, the legislative framework was expanded with a so called Law on the Help for Romanian Communities from Everywhere (Romanian Parliament 1998). It aimed to protect the rights of Romanian citizens abroad. Alongside this the Romanian government in 2002 established a recruitment system for jobs abroad. So Romanian emigration can not just be seen as a natural flow caused by push- or pull-factors. It's a more or less politically controlled exportation of workers.

Other countries, such as Germany, were waiting for the Romanian workers. Before the visa liberalizations free movement of workers was almost impossible within Europe. But the Western European countries found ways to open their borders, at least partially. Germany for instance opened its borders for low skilled – cheap – Romanian workers by signing bilateral agreements on workforce mobility. The earliest agreement between Germany and Romania was an agreement on contract construction workers in the early 1990s when Germany's construction sector was booming and there was a big demand for construction workers. Later on agreements for seasonal workers (agriculture, hotel and catering industry), 'guest workers' and housekeepers (de facto caregivers) were signed (Sachverständigenrat 2011). So Romania's emigration policy finds its counterpart in Germany's short term work migration policy. But the families of these workers have not been invited to Germany. So transnational families can be also seen as 'products' of a certain economic policy.

When Romania entered the European Union in 2007, Romanians became European citizens. When they were asked in 2011, what EU means for them personally, 56 percent of the Romanians answered, that EU meant for them the freedom to travel all over Europe (Sachverständigenrat 2013, 45). The Romanian researcher Dana Dimitrescu said, Romanians after 1989 had been "crazy to travel" (Dimitrescu 2013, 4). This is even more the case for the period from 2007 on. The political circumstances now allowed them to work legally all over Europe; even if there were some labour market restrictions in some countries. Romanians were free to choose the sector in which they wanted to work and the period they wanted to stay. In Germany they have full access to the labour market from 2014 onwards. European legislation guarantees equal rights in each EU country. So, theoretically it is easier to bring children over to the country where the parents found a job. But still many Romanians hesitate to do so. Others did and reversed their decision. The bad working conditions of many Romanian workers abroad do not enable them to provide housing and alimentation for their family members with them. Because of short term contracts or exploitative working conditions the income is not foreseeable, and leaving the children back home in many cases seems more secure.

Transnational Romanian Families

The information about transnational families is provided by the schools. A governmental decree of 2006 foresees a monitoring system for children with parents abroad (Agenția Națională pentru Protecția Drepturilor Copilului 2006). So in practice the teachers interview their pupils several times a year about their personal and family situation. Who of the parents left? Who takes care of the child? The data is transmitted to the district's Social Assistance Direction.

According to recent statistics provided by the National Agency for Child Protection there are 72,566 transnational families in Romania. That number includes families with one parent abroad (47,267), families with both parents abroad (15,385) and families with the single parent abroad (9,914). We talk about a number of 94,662 children who have at least one parent abroad. The quota of kids raised by other family members averages 94 percent. A number of 3,571 children (4 percent) is categorized as a group at risk and therefore integrated in the state's child protection program (Agenția Națională pentru Protecția Drepturilor Copilului 2016).

In 2013 the Romanian government resigned the law on child protection. It introduced a new paragraph which obligates parents to announce their departure within 40 days at the local authorities. In the case that both parents depart or the only parent departs, it is necessary to authorize an adult family member to take care of the child(ren) left back home. Their full access to social rights could be guaranteed only under such conditions, the authorities are arguing. And as social workers report the departure without announcement can be a big problem. If the grandmother is not officially authorized, she can not sign in the name of the parents and the child can not participate at certain activities such as after school programs or holiday camps and the family cannot benefit from of social assistance. But many migrants ignore this direction. If anybody ever got the punishment of 500 - 1,000 RON (110 - 220€), is not clear.

In most of the cases the child stays with the other parent or the grandparents. But there is a gender aspect: if the father leaves, the child remains with the mother. But if the mother leaves, in more of the cases it stays with grandmother. In rural areas, where most of the transnational migrants come from, the gender roles are still 'traditional'. Men are not used to be responsible for the care work, so they do not actively take over the responsibilities of the mother, if she left. It is true also in other parts of the world, that migration became feminine. More women find work in the care sector, especially in the domiciliary care of older people. So the care work at home, which is traditionally done by women, is done by other women; in some cases by migrant women. Researchers call this "care chains" (Rohr & Rau 2012).

In general the forms families organize their lives differ a lot. Of course, this happens not necessarily under the eyes of the state – so numbers do not show the whole picture. As for instance a social worker from Dorohoi reported the case of a monoparental family which organizes working abroad and caregiving for the child like shift work. While the mother is in Italy, the grandma stays with the child.

After three months they are swapping their responsibilities (Vogel 2013, 42).

Besides the double burden for the women – caring for the family at home and earning money abroad – one should also take a closer look on the fathers. Some of them have lost their jobs already in the 1990s. Some of these men have jobs but do not earn enough money to feed the family, which is considered to be their main responsibility. The minimum wage in Romania was about 319€ in 2017. And many of Romanian workers do not get higher payment, because politicians and investors handle it as a reference wage. The traditional role of fathers in Romania is in distress. Not all do get along with this. Some start to drink alcohol, some retire or suffer from depression. Some commit suicide.

We need to widen the perspective. Grandparents, the partner and other family members are not just important in their role for the child left behind by one or both parents. If we talk about transnational Romanian families, we need to take into account, that the departure of one or more family members changes the whole system. Each member of the family – taking care of the child or not – will be influenced somehow by the situation.

What work migration means for relationships and marriages is still not clear. Investigations need to be done. Statistics would help to get an overview. How to cope with the absence of the partner? What can I do, if my wife or husband starts a new life in Italy, Spain, Germany, ... – without me? Many Romanian citizens are confronted with these questions. And it can be supposed, that transnational migration

leads to a break of marriages in many cases. What on the other hand can mean a growing number of international marriages. Transnational migration changes traditional forms of 'family'.
And it is also about the situation of Romania's elderly population. In many cases they live in old rural houses without electricity, water lines and canalization. They do not want to leave the place where they were born. Some still work in the agriculture while others became 'parents' again, taking care of their grandchildren. Some grandparents are in need of a caregiver themselves. Taking care of one or more children means a physical and mental overload for many of them. Homework, feeding, washing, shopping brings grandparents to their limits.

Panettone, Smart Phones, Houses and Money: Objects of Transnationality

"After a while, good things started to happen: the most beautiful toys in the world showed up in the house and my mother bought us new clothes, new shoes and wonderful pink backpacks", remembers the Romanian journalist Lina Vdovîi (Vdovîi 2016, 123), who originates from Moldova. Her father after working in several fields found a job in Israel.

Children left behind are told very often, that their parents left for their better future. The material messages from abroad are to be understood as proofs of their parents' love. Finding and sending all kinds of things for their children is the second job of mothers and fathers abroad. So, after working 14 hours 6 days a week as a cleaner, caregiver, harvest helper or construction worker they switch to the 'real' job: to contact and feed their children.

Tons of Panettone,[3] fruits, sweets, dresses, barbies, shoes and toys cross the Romanian border each year. Most of the busses circulating between Spain, Italy, Belgium, France, Germany, Austria and Romania have huge trailers behind them. Furniture, bicycles, computers, textiles, building materials are sent to the village of origin in Romania. The objects embody the wish of parents to show their love – and their economic success in the foreign country.

"I want to make my house like in Italy, with wall and floor tiles, not the way it looked before. It should be like in Italy," says a migrant worker from the northern Romanian village Borşa (Schneider 2016, 18). Building houses plays an important role for transnational migrants, shows the impressive travelling exhibition *Brave New World – Romanian Migrants' Dream Houses* by Raluca Betea and Beate Wild. The houses – in some cases even palaces – symbolize the migrants' wish to come 'home'. The construction work takes years, a lot of money is invested. It has to be like in 'the West'. But it will never be like that, because the rural area where most of the new houses are built does not provide a corresponding infrastructure like canalization, water lines, electricity or paved roads. No one lives in these houses – because of lacking infrastructure and because the owners work and live abroad. The future is empty, rural Romania is full of widespread, oversized, modern ghost houses.

3 Panettone is a traditional Italian christmas and new years' cake.

The goods parents send from abroad – precursors of a brighter future – function as substitutes. It is not only the children suffering from being separated from their parents, it is also the other way around. So for parents, even if they can not be physically close to their child, the sending of presents is a strategy to compensate the separation. Through presents the parents can be present in their child's life, at least for a moment.

Of course, the emotional deprivation can not be recouped by sending soft toys. Social workers from Romania report that the younger the child is, the harder it understands and copes with its mothers and /or fathers emigration. More than ten years ago the Romanian government together with the NGO *Social Alternatives* started a campaign to sensitize future migrants for the need of a good and adequate communication with the child (Luca 2009). Communication can prevent more of the emotional stress than materials can compensate afterwards.

The Romanian researcher Anamaria Iuga conducted a study on objects that 'travel' between the country of origin and the host societies. She found that Romanians living in Spain counteracted the absence of their native village and their relatives by practicing their native lifestyle and even bringing items of traditional furniture to their new homes abroad. Carpets, blankets, pillowcases from rural areas in Romania, as well as traditional clothing is transported to Western European countries in order to keep the memories alive. Iuga observed a "cultural dialogue between two radically different communities with distinct values and distinct cultural specificity" (Iuga 2016, 116).

Not directly visible but with huge influence are the money flows between the diaspora and the families in Romania. In 2016 around 3 Billion Euros in remittances were sent to Romania from other countries. The biggest money flows came from Italy (1.02 Billion Euro), Spain (806 Million Euro) and Germany (456 Million Euro). Even if the rate of the remittances is slightly decreasing, they are still a very important factor of Romania's economy. Remittances are used to construct or repair the house (96 percent of Romanians are home owners!), to send children to school or university, to pay health care costs or grandma's caregiver. With their money migrants keep the stumbling Romanian public sector alive.

Conclusion

"Money doesn't bring happiness", concludes a dramatic portrait of children with parents abroad, broadcasted by the Romanian television TVR some years ago. These children suffer a lot, they are raised by telephone or video chat and their parents do not understand their real situation, it is said. Some of these presumptions may be true, but the picture of 'the abandoned of today' lacks of seriosity. "The parents have the right to travel and work everywhere. The children, injured souls, have the right to suffer," ends the short documentary (TVR 2016).

Voices like that can be found easily in Romania's public discourse. The Romanian journalist Lina Vdovîi considers the dramatization as an exaggeration. She herself is the child of migrant parents. She writes about the positive aspects in the lives of transnational families. She talked to her colleagues, friends – all with migrant family background – and found that: "for us, being left behind was an opportunity to thrive" (Vdovîi 2016, 119).

Empiric data on the positive aspects of transnational migration on the left behind children is still limited but there are some incidents that children with parents abroad become independent earlier, they take over responsibility for their lives and that one of their (younger) brothers and /or sisters more easily, they learn to run a household, they learn how to use computers and other communication technology and the material and financial help from abroad strengthens their self-confidence. Materials for school, books and university fees in many cases would not be affordable without some extra money – which is in fact not 'extra' but the main source of income of many Romanian families.

So the phenomenon of Romanian transnational families is a quite ambivalent one. By sending money and goods Romanian migrants keep the economic, health care and educational system going. On the other hand the exodus of thousands of Romanians each year hits the social system even more. Romania looses taxes, brains and population.

From a more global perspective transnational families are a short term phenomenon, that will occur as long as the countries of destination are not providing conditions for the migrants to bring their families and as long as huge income inequalities force people to enter labour markets beyond their countries' borders. It is a symptom of global and European social inequalities. Hopefully they will equalize more and more, so the future world of the "children of global migration" (Parreñas 2005) will look different.

References

Agenția Națională pentru Protecția Drepturilor Copilului. 15/06/2006. "Ordinul nr. 219/2006 privind activitățile de identificare, intervenție și monitorizare a copiilor care sunt lipsiți de ingrijirea părinților pe perioada în care aceștia se află la muncă în străinătate." In *Monitorul oficial al României*.

Agenția Națională pentru Protecția Drepturilor Copilului. 2016. "Situație copii cu părinți plecați la muncă in străinătate." In *MinisterulMuncii, Familiei, Protecției Sociale i Persoanelor V.rstnice*. Online available here: http://www.copii.ro/statistici/, last verified at 18/02/2018.

Brunner, Kati; Sawka, Marjana; Onufriv, Sofia (Eds.). 2013. *Skype mama*. Berlin: Ed. fotoTAPETA.

Cărtărescu, Mircea. 2014. *Die Flügel. Roman*. Wien: Zsolnay, Paul, p. 282.

Copii singuri acasa. 2016. Campania TVR "România copiilor singuri acasă." Portret de țara. Online available here: http://copiisinguriacasa.ro/pentru-parinti/ce-poti-face-pentru-copil/campania-tvr-romania-copiilor-singuri-acasa/, last verified at 17/02/2018.

Diefenbach, Andrea; Crudu, Dumitru; Vieru, Grigore; Abé, Nicola. 2013. *Land Ohne Eltern*.[Country without parents]. Heidelberg, London: Kehrer; Turnaround.

Dimitrescu, Dana, cited by Anghel, Remus Gabriel. 2013. *Romanians in Western Europe. Migration, status dilemmas, and transnational connections*. Plymouth: Lexington Books, p. 4.

Iuga, Anamaria. 2016. "Objects that travel with emigrants from Maramureș." In Raluca Betea und Beate Wild (Eds.): *Brave new world. Romanian migrants' dream houses*, pp. 106–117, p. 116.

Luca, Catalin. 2009. *Ghid pentru părinții care pleacă la muncă în străinătate*. Ed. by Alternative Sociale. Editura Terra Nostra.

Manu, Sorin. 2010. *Home alone: A Romanian Tragedy*.

Parreñas, Rhacel Salazar. 2005. *Children of Global Migration. Transnational Families and Gendered Woes*. Stanford University Press.

Rohr, Elisabeth; Rau, Elin. 2012. Transnationale Kindheit und die care chain-Debatte. In Carmen Brikle (Ed.) *Emanzipation und feministische Politiken. Verwicklungen, Verwer-

fungen, Verwandlungen, 4th
ed. Ulrike Helmer Verlag.
Romanian Parliament.15/07/1998.
*Lege nr. 150 / 1998 privind
acordarea de sprijin
comunităților românești de
pretutindeni.* Online available
here http://www.legex.ro/
Legea-150-1998-15269.aspx,
last verified at 23/06/2017.
Sachverständigenrat deutscher
Stiftungen für Integration und
Migration. 2011. *Migrations-
land 2011. Jahresgutachten
2011 mit Migrationsbaro-
meter,* pp. 82-87.
Sachverständigenrat deutscher
Stiftungen für Integration und
Migration. 2013. *Erfolgsfall
Europa? Folgen und Heraus-
forderungen der EU-Freizü-
gigkeit für Deutschland.
Jahresgutachten 2013 mit
Migrationsbarometer,* p. 45.

Sandu, Dumitru. 2000.
"Migrația circulatorie ca
strategie de viața." In
Sociologie Româneasca
(2), pp. 5–29.
Schneider, Xaver Victor. 2016.
"Exhibition Concept." In
Raluca Betea und Beate
Wild (Eds.): *Brave new world.
Romanian migrants' dream
houses,* pp. 10–39, p. 18.
Șerban, Florin. 2010. *If I want
to whistle, I whistle.*
Vdovîi, Lina. 2016. The
"Left-Behind Kids are Alright."
In Raluca Betea und Beate
Wild (Eds.): *Brave new
world. Romanian migrants'
dream houses,* p. 118–123
Vogel, Janka. 2013. *Transnationale
Familien in Rumänien. Die
Situation von Kindern und
Jugendlichen in Dorohoi, deren
Eltern im Ausland arbeiten.*

München: Grin Verlag, p.42.
Voltaj. 2015. *De la capăt.*
[All over again.] Online available here: https://www.
youtube.com/watch?v=
WA3wOKHpzEU, last
verified at 21/05/2015.

The tensions, conflicts, and psychological ramifications engendered by the separation of parents and children in the *Gastarbeiter* generation, the so-called guest workers in Germany, were taboo subjects and ignored for many years not only by those affected but also in the political sphere. In *Generation Suitcase: The Children Left Behind* (2011) Gülcin Wilhelm encapsulates for the first time the topic 'suitcase children' in its political and psychological aspects, focusing on the child's perspective. To date, this book is the sole publication that comprehensively tackles this thematic.

Generation Suitcase

The Children Left Behind

Gülcin Wilhelm

"It is a macabre fact that ultimately it was the migrant workers from Turkey themselves who harmed their children, for whose well-being and secure future they had come to Germany at that time," comments a Berlin-based psychotherapist of Turkish origin.

These are the children who, as babies or as infants, were left behind in Turkey by their parents, who themselves had emigrated to Germany to work, and who later, in the period between 1975 and 1985, were fetched by their parents. For some of these so-called suitcase children, a state of uncertainty persisted for years, for they were sent back and forth between Germany and Turkey for a multitude of reasons.

Only a few of those left behind as children in Turkey seem to have a degree of understanding for their parents' devotion and self-sacrifice. If we scrutinize the conditions under which the Turkish first-generation migrants lived and worked in Germany, it is difficult at first to fathom their lack of understanding. Are their children being unfair? Are they ungrateful daughters and sons, for whom the parents worked to acquire land and shops in their homeland? Life itself furnishes this answer – and it is no simple answer; it would imply that the so-called generation suitcase is disloyal or even bears malice. And yet, it is obvious that the fundamental trust of these children in the two people in whom they had most relied had been shaken.

Labour Recruitment Agreement and Family Reunion

Given that the Federal Republic of Germany urgently needed manpower in its effort to rebuild in the post-war years, labour recruitment agreements were signed with Turkey and other Mediterranean countries. Family reunion by migrant workers from Turkey was not per se desirable in Germany. The first proof of this can be witnessed in the 1961 agreement between Germany and Turkey [...]. In addition to the passage, which stipulated that those who came to Germany to work should be single, both signatory states agreed that family members were not allowed to relocate to Germany. While the 1973 recruitment ban for foreign workers affected Greek, Italian, Spanish, and Turkish migrants in equal measure, restrictions on family reunion applied specifically to workers from Turkey. For example, Germany's 1955 treaty with the Italian state allowed migrant workers to fetch family members on condition that they had adequate accommodation. Following this prototype, recruitment agreements were signed with Greece and Spain in 1960.

Reuniting children, wives and husbands of migrant workers from Turkey, however, did not fit into the German government's concept. The then Turkish government, in turn, was more than content to be rid of just under 800,000 people in one fell swoop; this relieved pressure on its own labour market, while at the same time ensuring that substantial sums of foreign currency would flow back into the country. Against the background of these mutual interests, both states could be satisfied with the agreement. They were utterly indifferent to the needs of those affected by it, however.

The recruitment agreement between Germany and Turkey also incorporated a so-called rotation principle, according to which the duration of stay by Turkish workers in Germany should be limited. This was to be the basis for the status of 'guest worker'; its objective was to respond flexibly to the labour market's needs in order to, where necessary, either recruit new migrant workers or repatriate 'dispensable' workers. The rotation plan, however, proved unrealistic and thus not applicable. Eventually, it had to be abolished.

This precarious situation, however, only exerted limited influence on the overwhelming majority of migrant workers from Turkey in deciding not to bring their families to Germany at that juncture. Their life plan was such that they had envisaged a speedy return to their homeland. Their intention was to earn as much money as possible in as short a time as possible, and save as much as possible in order to ensure an existence for themselves in Turkey thereafter. Following this rationale, each additional person in the household would have entailed extra costs, so it was actually better for family members to remain behind in Turkey.

German Immigration Policy and its Ramifications

The process of the final settlement for the workforce from Turkey had meanwhile slowly begun. Participants could not and did not want to take note of this creeping development at the time – at best, it is recognizable in retrospect. By 1972, 21% of migrants from Turkey had already been in Germany for more than seven years and hence were entitled to acquire a residence permit (cf Pagenstecher 1995). Their housing situation was also undergoing a change; whereas previously they were forced to live in workers' homes and residential barracks, in 1972 around half of them were tenants of a self-contained apartment (cf ibid.).

The end of the recruitment campaign came about in 1973. Germany no longer had any need for foreign workers, who for about fifteen years had helped drive the German economy to its apogee. After the global oil crisis erupted, the afflicted industries started laying off employees. The boom times were over. The then ruling coalition of Social Democrats (SDP) and Free Democrats (FDP) finally imposed a recruitment ban on 'guest workers,' which impacted all countries with which Germany had signed a labour recruitment agreement. This triggered a wave of family reunions: migrants – from Turkey, who had a residence permit, brought their wives and children to Germany. The worry that they would never be allowed to enter Germany again due to the recruitment ban had the effect of making them reconsider their plans to return to their homeland. For the most part, this led to a somewhat more sedentarism. From 3.9 million at the time of the recruitment ban, the foreign population rose to 4.5 million by 1989 (see Hoffmann 1992).

In 1973, some 900,000 Turkish citizens lived in Germany. Owing to measures to curb fresh immigration, additional restrictions were imposed for migrants from Turkey. According to a new regulation, family members, for example, entering Germany after 30 November 1974 would no longer receive a work permit. The deadline for work permits for adolescent migrants was deferred until 31 December 1976, however. This extension was due to the fact that young people were brought to Germany on a massive scale in the wake of the recruitment ban and the cuts in family allowance (see below), and these young people should also be allowed access to the employment- and training-vacancy markets. In 1974, 31% of all foreign children under the age of fifteen were of Turkish descent (cf Schober 1981).

Cuts in Family Allowance

As of January 1975, family allowances for children of Turkish migrants living in Turkey were to be significantly cut, triggering an even greater wave of family reunions than in 1973 and 1974. Up to the point when these cuts were implemented, family members from the recruiting countries received 10 German Marks (DM) for the first child, 25 DM for the second, 60 DM for the third, and 70 DM for the fourth and each additional child per month as child benefit – irrespective of whether the children were living in Germany or elsewhere. This principle was conceived in the 1960s so as to incentivise "guest workers." As of 1975, the full child allowance was now only to be paid to those children living in Germany. No reliable information is available as to how many of the estimated 700,000 children living in Turkey were ultimately impacted by family allowance cuts, triggering their parents to decide to bring them to Germany.

Emigration in the Wake of the Military Putsch

The number of migrants from Turkey grew between 1978 and 1981; in particular the military putsch in 1980 triggered many of those politically persecuted to emigrate to Germany. The political upheavals in Turkey during this period, which at times involved armed intervention, contributed to parents' deciding to bring their children to Germany. Their concern for the wellbeing and lives of their children prompted yet another wave of family reunions. By 1980, 90% of migrants from Turkey already lived in a self-contained apartment (cf Pagenstecher 1995). The number of those entitled to a residence permit due to their seven-year stay in the Federal Republic of Germany was 76.6% (see ibid.). The proportion of Turkish children under the age of fifteen, of the total number of foreign children living in Germany, was 46% (see Schober 1981).

Lowering the Age-Limit for Children to enter Germany

In 1981, a drastic amendment to the law in force, according to which the age-limit for children requiring a visa to enter Germany was lowered from eighteen to sixteen, sparked off the next big wave of family reunions. This law came into effect shortly before the Christian Democrat (CDU)-Free Democrat (FDP) coalition were to replace the incumbent SDP/FDP government. Immediately after the arrival of children in Germany on a massive scale, a persistent phase continued until 1986, during which more Turkish nationals emigrated from the Federal Republic of Germany than immigrated. This was mainly due to the fact that as of 1981 new provisions for migrants from Turkey rendered it difficult for spouses to come to Germany. Since 1986, from when there has been more immigration than emigration from Germany, the increase in the Turkish resident population has mainly been due to a rise in birth rates (cf Kramer 1988).

Payment to encourage Reverse Migration

The afore-mentioned lowering of the age limit was preceded by another attempt to limit migration from Turkey, which was also due to policies implemented by the SPD/FDP government. If until circa 1978 the maxim "temporary integration" hinged upon the migrants' voluntary return, non-EEC nationals were henceforth offered a premium that would incentivize their "voluntary" return. The measure, the implementation of which was entrusted to the incoming government, targeted in particular migrants from Turkey, who had become unemployed due to company restructuring. In the event of their definitive repatriation, accompanied by their entire family, returnees would be paid a premium of DM 10,500, in addition to DM 1,500 per child. The offer, which was valid from October 1983 to June 1984, also provided for reimbursing the migrants' pension contributions – with retention of the employer's contribution. Ultimately, however, only a few migrants availed of the possibility to receive this premium. Contrary to the then available official date, which referred to 300,000 returnees, the actual figure was only 133,000 including family members (cf Hönekopp 1987). In 1985, the proportion of migrants from Turkey in possession of a residence permit was 85.1% (cf Pagenstecher 1995). At that juncture the process of family reunion was largely settled for them. [...]

Dilemma for those Left Behind

[The 'Kofferkinder' or 'Pendelkinder,' [literally, pendulum children] thematic remains a taboo – presumably even one of the most serious and harrowing among the migrant community. This taboo directly impacts almost every single migrant family from Turkey. The topic remains a taboo for those left behind and for their parents alike.]

The tabooing of the issue by those affected, who bear scars from their early childhood separation, stems from a dilemma. Those left behind blame their parents, or at least one of them, for their misfortunes. They feel justified in their immense rage and hardly seem willing to forgive. And yet, it has been observed that they tend to set aside their own painful experiences when it comes to questioning their parents' actions critically. Furthermore, Turkish social norms play a critical role, whereby great importance is placed upon obedience. The educational norms shaped by these values often render critical dialogue about the past by those affected with their parents nigh on impossible. In order not to appear as unfair among family members and in the community, those affected shy away from making accusations in public. [...]

Those affected often feel a loathing for those properties in Turkey that have been procured for them, but over which they cannot voice their feelings so comfortably. Instead, they feel compelled to acknowledge the efforts behind all their parents' sacrifices.

The topic of money is closely linked to the tabooing of the problem. Those left behind as children find it difficult to accept that their parents, and especially that their mother, did not want them at their side because of money.

Guilt or shame also hampers those affected from talking openly about what they have experienced. They remain tight-lipped, for they are afraid of how they themselves might react, should someone pass a negative comment about their parents. [...]

Parental Motives

Before grappling with the causes of why parents left their children with relatives, or didn't bring them to Germany, or had them commute to and fro between Germany and Turkey, one certainty must be reckoned with: no mother leaves her child flippantly or carelessly. No parent voluntarily ventures into the unknown, leaving family and homestead behind. This predicament was triggered by the Turkish state, which did not adequately provide for its citizens, thus compelling them to emigrate. As for the German state, from the outset it insisted on the rotation principle, whereby migrant workers swiftly return to Turkey, and they didn't initiate the creation of suitable living conditions that would have bolstered family cohesion. At first glance, this did not necessarily run contrary to the migrants' life-planning; they had anticipating staying in Germany for an average of two years. Even were they to change their minds, however, and wanted to stay longer with their families, family-friendly apartments were extremely rare: "The sole obstacle to family reunion was the housing problem ... Most migrant families moved into cheap condemned buildings in the big cities' older neighbourhoods, where they were welcomed as 'rotating' temporary dwellers by the urban redevelopment agencies" (cf ibid.).

While these facts furnish an explanation for the challenging conditions under which parents had to make a decision, for those affected these reasons aren't enough to explain away their depressing life without their parents.

From conversations with people left behind as children, as well as with experts in the field, we can sum up by stating that the time-spans, during which parents contemplated whether to fetch their children or not, can be divided into three distinct phases:

The First Phase

The first phase is determined by the fact that migrants didn't settle permanently in Germany or that official government policy actively supported them to return to Turkey. Were children to settle with their parents in Germany, then the project that migrants swiftly return could not be realized. If parents were considering whether to fetch their children or not, concrete obstacles such as the failing and costly day-care places, or undignified housing conditions were not paramount.

Rather, the decisive factors were individual life plans about returning to Turkey; a successful return was contingent upon saving as much money as possible. Every child living with them in Germany, and not in Turkey, would have entailed more costs, and that would have delayed implementing the goal of returning. Only very few migrants could fulfil the dream of returning to Turkey at the desired time with sufficient savings. The vast majority ultimately settled in Germany.

The decision to leave the children behind in Turkey hinged upon the idea that it would not be worthwhile taking them 'for a few years'. Yet, 'a few years' turned into five years, and five years turned into twenty. In most cases parents did not recognize or even perceive the harm that these first 'few years' had already inflicted on the children left behind. They underestimated the importance of such a timespan for the psyche of a child, and tended not to take the emotional burden this engendered fully to heart. As they saw it, the children would surely be in safe hands with their grandmother. They were sending the children money and they wouldn't starve.

The Second Phase

The second phase commences with the tentative process by migrants from Turkey to establish themselves in Germany. During this period, many parents' deliberations on whether they should bring their children to Germany or not were equally as tentative. Plans to return to Turkey someday were far from being abandoned. So issues concerning the children remained mostly in the background. Money transfers had meanwhile assumed another form. While it had always been a case of saving enough, now it was called 'a little bit more'. This 'a little bit more' also related to how long the migrants stayed in Germany. For the children, this attitude again meant that they would remain behind in Turkey. Given that in some instances the children were already at school, many parents felt that it was now too late for a change anyway.

As of 1975 changes in family allowance for children living outside of Germany impacted the parents' decision-making process. For a family of three or four, the difference was enormous. While benefits for children living in Turkey remained the same as beforehand, the amount for those living in Germany – depending on their number – saw a two- to five-fold increase. How many children were brought from Turkey to Germany as a result of this change is not statistically proven, however. This much is certain: according to the department responsible for child benefits (*Familienkasse*) at the Federal Labour Office, a total of 1,928,000 foreign children were in receipt of child benefit in 1975.

According to the Social Policy Review of the Press and Information Office of the Federal Government, 762,000 of those children were living in Turkey at that time. It is generally assumed that over the course of restructuring child benefits (1975), as well as changes in regulations for residence permits (1978); some 700,000 children were reunited with their families in Germany (cf Hopf 1981).

The Third Phase

The last phase, linked to the decision by the SPD/FDP government in 1981 to reduce the age limit for children entering Germany from eighteen to sixteen, was experienced by many migrant children as a different kind of tragedy: constantly commuting between Germany and Turkey. Those affected were children, who initially had been brought to Germany for good, as well as those who had to commute from time to time, irregularly or following the rhythm of their respective school holidays. Over the course of conversations preceding the publication of *Generation Suitcase. The Children Left Behind* (Wilhelm, 2011) it came to light that some of those affected could no longer trace back when, how often, and how long they stayed in Germany and Turkey. From today's perspective, the rationale behind sending children back and forth cannot always be understood.

Generally, children had no say in the matter; they only brought influence to bear insofar as they had to be sent back if they were suffering so intensely from the separation from their long-time caretakers in Turkey that they could no longer stand it in Germany. Otherwise, children were sent back and forth for a multitude of reasons. If the parents had settled permanently in Germany, they often justified their decision to send the children back to Turkey owing to the prevailing traditional values in Turkey. Girls in particular were taken out of school in the middle of the academic year and returned to the care of relatives in their homeland. These children and adolescents ought not forget their Turkishness; they were sent to Turkey to get back in touch with their roots and to internalize the corresponding moral standards. The children ought not or no longer come into contact with such things as sex education, with the West's 'reprehensible morals' and in general, with everything that was 'German' in their view. The decisive factor for this attitude was the parents' national consciousness; religion, however, didn't yet have the significance that it has today. Nevertheless, there were also those parents, as reported by Safter Çınar, migration representative of the German Trade Union Confederation, who subsequently regretted having sent their children back to Turkey. They themselves brought their children back and often desperately sought support so that their

children could keep up with the pace of German schools, which was sometimes no longer possible.

Until 1997/ 1998, when visa requirements or the residence permit requirements for children under the age of sixteen was introduced, Turkish parents enjoyed a certain 'freedom' when it came to registering and de-registering their children and even children of relatives in Germany. Many also brought their nieces to Germany, partly to give them better educational opportunities and partly to use them in childcare. [...]

The emotional and psychological consequences of uprootedness linked to migration are more devastating for those who didn't voluntarily come to Germany than for those who themselves opted to come. The erstwhile 'suitcase children', who were left behind, belong to the first group. While most migrants face stigma and prejudice, those who could not choose for themselves also grapple with the impact of losing their identities, amplified due to the trauma they've endured. Those affected lost a part of themselves, which led to a splintering of their identity.

References

Hoffmann, Lutz. 1992. *Die unvollendete Republik. Zwischen Einwanderungsland und deutschem Nationalstaat.* Köln: PapyRossa, p. 23

Hopf, Diether. 1981. "Schulprobleme der Ausländerkinder." In *Zeitschrift für Pädagogik,* 27 (1981) 6, p. 841

Hönekopp, Elmar. 1987. *Rückkehrförderung und die Rückkehr ausländischer Arbeitnehmer und ihrer Familien.* Institut für Arbeitsmarkt- und Berufsforschung Nürnberg

Kramer, Heinz. 1988. *Die Europäische Gemeinschaft und die Türkei.* Baden-Baden: Nomos, p. 220

Pagenstecher, Cord. 1995. "Die ungewollte Einwanderung. Rotationsprinzip und Rückkehrerwartung in der deutschen Ausländerpolitik." *In Geschichte in Wissenschaft und Unterricht,* 46 (12), pp. 718-737

Schober, Karin. 1981. "Zur Ausbildungs- und Arbeitsmarktsituation ausländischer Jugendlicher in der Bundesrepublik Deutschland." In: *Mitteilungen aus der Arbeitsmarkt- und Berufsforschung 1/81,* p. 13

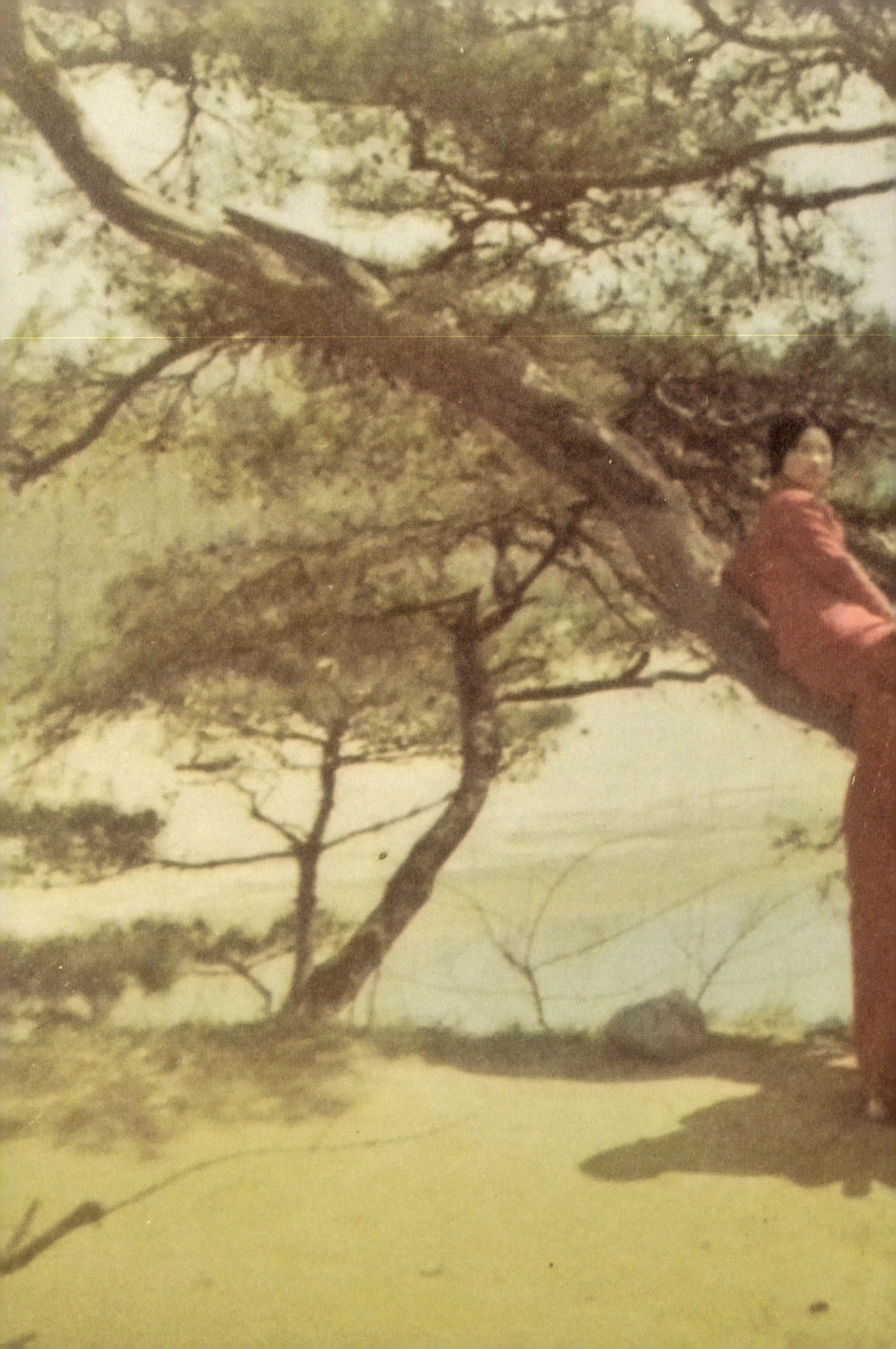

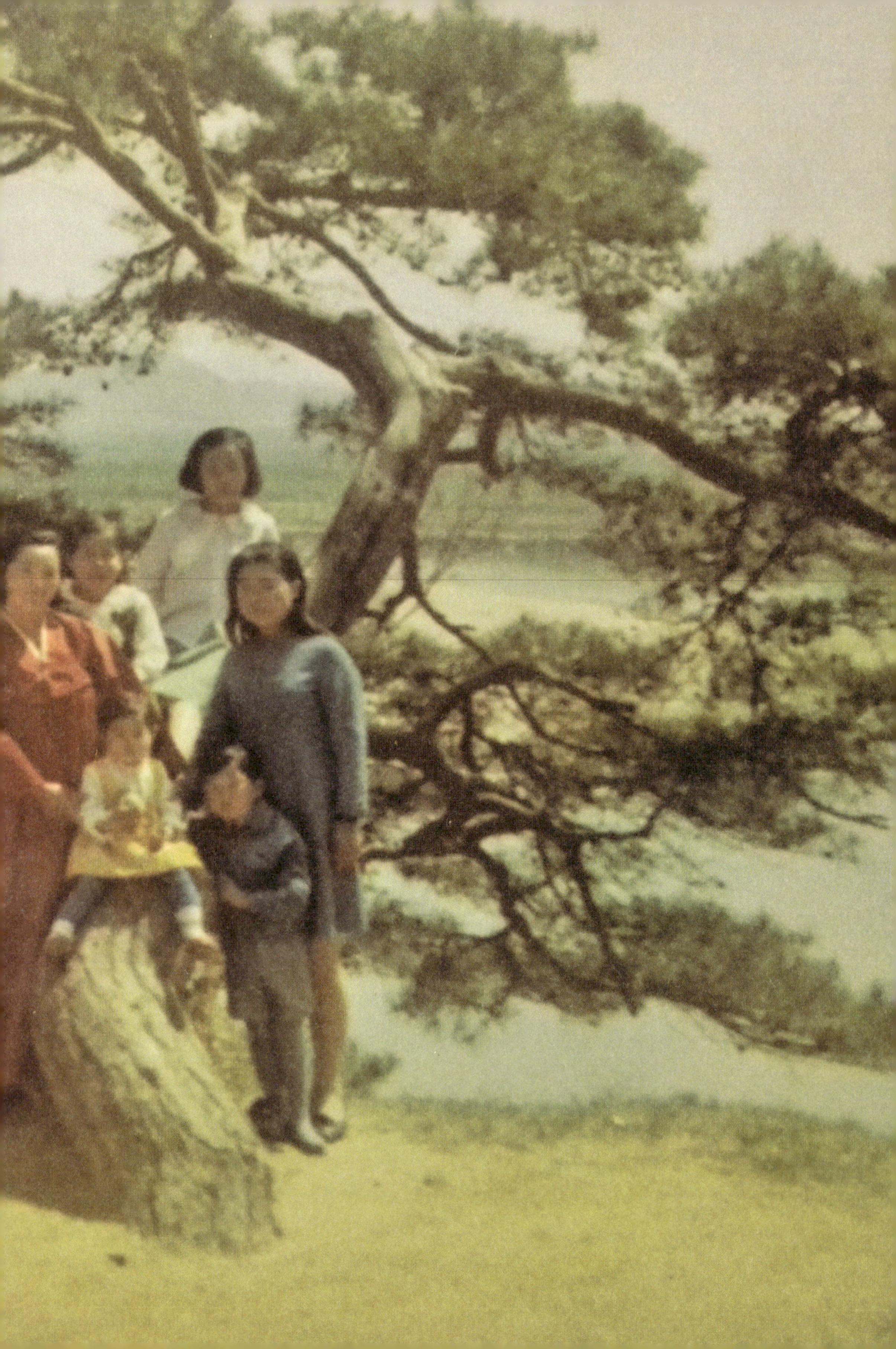

In the 1980s, Maria Papoulias first employed the term *Kofferkinder*
[suitcase children] to describe children left behind by their parents or
those who commuted between countries. This term is still used in the
context of the so-called guest workers from the 1960s to 1980s in the
then West-Germany. Papoulias' contribution addresses the psychological
ramifications of family separation for parents and children alike. The
text should be regarded as a historical contribution, and yet, the problem
of psychopathological reactions within transnational families is still
highly relevant today.

Suitcase Children

**Mother–child separation as a cause
of psychopathological reactions
among migrant workers families**

Maria Papoulias

In almost every third family of Greek labour migrants in the Federal Republic of Germany (FRG)[1] at least one child has been moved back and forth several times between Greece and Germany. In exchanging experiences with colleagues, I have been able to confirm that something similar also occurs in migrant workers families among other nationalities. The reason behind this mother-child separation is the mother's work practices. Her first child is sent back as early as its infant years to her native land to live with relatives. Following the birth of the second child, either the mother gives up her job, or because she is better informed due to her longer stay in Germany about accommodation facilities for her children, the second child usually does not experience the same fate and might remain with his or her parents in Germany from birth.

This mother-child separation, which takes place as early as in the infant years, has devastating effects on the future shape of the mother-child relationship. If, at a later stage, these children are brought back to Germany, insurmountable difficulties often emerge in communicating and building relationships with their parents. Psychopathological reactions on both sides are not uncommon; such families seek help from educational counsellors, or are in need of even more serious, psychiatric treatment. In this paper, I would like to describe this situation schematically, as it has crystallized in my own professional practice, as well as through discussions with colleagues, who have made comparable observations. These children, whom I generically refer to as 'suitcase children' – they are taken away at will and without regard to their emotional needs and then brought back, like suitcases that are constantly being moved about – often have attachment and behavioural difficulties linked to their 'inability to take root.'

How the Mother experiences Separation

Given that such a mother-child separation is not common in the traditional Greek family context, Greek mothers experience this life-constraining condition with feelings of guilt about being a bad mother, with a strained relationship with her husband, as well as with psychosomatic complaints. The prospect of financially securing their child's future through her own gainful employment merely superficially compensates for the emotional deficits and guilt caused by the separation from her child. Furthermore, this separation takes place during the early phase of the mother's stay in Germany, namely, at a time in which the young mother still has to withstand homesickness and has not yet acquired sufficient information or reference points

---

1 TN: At the time this article was published Germany was divided: the Federal Republic of Germany (FRG), to which this article refers, and the German Democratic Republic (DDR). For simplicity's sake, the term Germany is employed.

in her new environment. It moreover generates an ambivalent situation with regard to her relatives back in Greece – predominantly grandparents – where the child is being raised, on the one hand of gratitude for and commitment to the task undertaken, and, on the other, envy because the grandparents are the main reference persons for the child, and emotionally receive from the child that which parents consider to be their due.

How the Child processes Separation

Children cannot fathom the material reasons for this separation. They develop fantasies of 'abandonment', of 'being unwanted', of 'being the less loved' than younger siblings, who were always allowed to live permanently with their parents. The caregivers for those children, who stayed behind in Greece, are the relatives with whom they grow up. The child mostly calls them "Dad" and "Mom". The birth parents thus slip into the role of uncle and aunt, who appear on the scene once a year, with loads of clothes and toys from abroad. Younger children become perplexed by adults who suddenly appear from out of nowhere and make emotional demands, to which they are unable to reciprocate. Due to an educational predicament, relatives often portray the biological parents as bogeymen: "Just you wait until your father telephones, and then I'll have something to tell him!" All these circumstances contribute to the reality that children left behind in Greece rarely get the opportunity to develop a realistic, affirmative relationship with their birth parents. They experience their parents, as they themselves depict them, as "mythical beings, who appear from time to time, and then disappear again into the unknown."

Difficulties on reuniting with the Family

Children are sent to Germany, either because more favourable living conditions have now been created for them, or because the grandparents have become sick and elderly and can no longer cope with the growing child. In each case, being separated from these first caregivers entails a significant loss for the child. Many children find it difficult to move away from their familiar environment and relocate very grudgingly to their parents in Germany. This relocation to a foreign land, to blood parents with whom there's no deep bond, represents an intense psychological burden for the child. It is challenging for these children to spontaneously and lovingly engage with these unknown parents right away. The parents, in turn, feel neglected and hurt by the child's reluctance, which they interpret as rejection. Given that they have not participated in the child's development, parents are confronted from one day to the next with a being whose habits and reactions are not always comprehensible to them. They try to break the child's reserve by dint of forced behaviour. If they don't succeed in changing the child's responses, they experience that their parental authority has been questioned and resort to countermeasures, which, in turn, provoke unwanted reactions from the child. With overly emotional expectations and demands, "we are your parents, you ought to love us," they achieve the opposite and only reinforce the child's tendency to retreat, thus creating an unnatural, tense situation for all involved, behind which lingers disappointment, bitterness, helplessness, and guilt. The dialogue between parent and child – given that there has been no real communication – is pursued on a symbolic level, in which the child communicates his needs and desires to his parents through symptom-formations. Regressive tendencies also play a role in this process because the child clings to the past in Greece and often idealizes living together with his or her grandparents. Finding themselves in a blind alley, the parents clumsily try to eradicate this phase of the child's past in the hope that the child will soon come to terms with its parents, when the attachment with the grandparents in earlier years is "forgotten." In this way, the child, who does not yet feel at home with its parents, renounces his past in order to please and be accepted by them; the child relinquishes a past that affords it a foothold in life and security, and now drifts in an emotional void. The mother faces insurmountable difficulties on the child's return to the family. Misunderstandings that arise from a lack of insight into the child's emotional state and reactions degenerate into outright educative power struggles. The mother becomes confused in her maternal role and feels as though rejected by her child. For this reason, she clings to her second child and thus sets sibling rivalry and envy in motion.

Psychosomatic complaints and depressive reactions occur more frequently in this phase for the mother. Often the 'suitcase children' then return to Greece to go to school after a stay with the family in Germany, and this second relocation temporarily cushions tensions within the family, and may even unconsciously fulfil this objective. The grandparents, however, are in no time overwhelmed by the child's difficulties at school and behavioural problems and abandon their role of guardian. The child returns a second time to his parents in Germany. Depending on the child's age and developmental stage in its separation from its mother, and on the return into family life, the starting points for conflicts and their processing options shift. The basic dynamics remain unchanged, however. Many young foreigners, who end up in psychiatry, have undergone a career as 'suitcase children'.

Timely psychological and pedagogical counselling and education for mothers about the difficulties to be encountered on the return of the child to Germany have proven prophylactic. Enlightened mothers are more likely to bring better understanding, patience, and empathy to facilitate the child's re-integration into family life. Sufficient childcare for infants would be an even more effective solution, so that this mother-child separation among emigrant families would not be necessary in the first instance!

They call us Gastarbeiter (1985) is a compilation of interviews conducted by author and journalist Georg Matzouranis between 1966 and 1974 with Greek migrant workers in the Federal Republic of Germany. Without family considerations being a deliberate focus in the conversations, the abandonment and subsequent reunion with children comes to the fore in many interviews. In addition to interviews on general living and working conditions, the surveys were also conducted during strikes by migrant workers in summer 1973.

They call us Gastarbeiter Georg Matzouranis

Munich, 1971
(I.T.)

I came to Germany in 1961, first to Hamburg. Just like all of us, I came because I couldn't find work with which I could feed my children.

I worked in the city, well in the city and in the village, and my wife in the fields. I also went out into the fields whenever I had time, even on Sundays, and yet there was nothing doing. Too much debts because of poverty and the children. I couldn't make up my mind whether to bring my family here.

I, whom you see in front of you, have profound troubles, but I keep them to myself. What troubles? Domestic, as they say; the separation has greatly affected me.

Especially now, that I'm not going to Greece. Don't interrupt me with the whys and wherefores. I'm not going; what more of an explanation do you want?

I work in the automobile industry. As a line and piecemeal worker. You've got to finish so many tasks within a certain time. If you cannot manage that, you'll earn less. These are the shenanigans of those here. You've to toil away until you go mad so as to get your pay. As a result, you can fall apart like my colleague and then take yourself to hospitals, just like he did. They say he suffered a nervous breakdown and that he's now twitching his nose; that's to say that he's a permanent grimace and can't control it.

Another co-worker, who was constantly watching out for when the next car would appear overhead so that he could attach a bolt, began to squint.

Repeating the identical task year after year drives you crazy. But poverty is poverty and you can't just simply quit the company. You've got to settle in again, no matter wherever you go, and everywhere is the same.

I live in a factory dorm; over 2,000 of us foreigners are living there; Turks, a few Spaniards, and Greeks. I pay 100 marks[2] rent a month, with four of us to a room. We don't quarrel; nevertheless, you can't live decently there. That's why we just go there to sleep. What should the others do to help you? Everyone has to wash his own clothes and cook something for himself. As for entertainment, it's limited, what more can I tell you. There's a *Kafenion*[3] nearby, and we spend our time there. I play cards there. I do that because what I earn from my work isn't enough for me. I know that's not right, especially for me, because many people from my village are

2 TN: The equivalent of 52€.

3 TN: A Greek café where people
socialise and play card games.

here, and they can observe me. I know many of them, because I was a bus driver in my village, and I know them all, including those from neighbouring villages. Some of them also don't talk to me, but I'm no professional card player; I play to win.

We have card players there who have made it their profession, and get others who haven't the slightest notion involved, in order to fleece them. Grigoris from Kilkis is permanently on sick leave, for he's playing cards and swanking around in a big car. He has his brother and brother-in-law and they ensnare fools. I went there too on the first day, but realized they were cheating and didn't go back afterwards so as not to end up in a knife fight. I have a family, a wife, and three children in Greece, and I have to send 600 marks a month; I've even more worries, that's why I play. If I lose, I undertake to make amends; and then I say: at least to get back what I just lost, because the other amused himself with my money in Themi's pub in the evening. I thought about heading to Hamburg if I go away from here; I'll surely get used to it, because as long as I'm living here, I let myself be tempted. I can't say no to those with whom I was playing yesterday. There are many tricks with card games, and I know them all, but I'm not on a winning roll. If ever I got on a roll, I would call it a day immediately – until the very end.

To tell you the truth, I'll only quit playing if I manage to bring my family here. But I don't know how to carry that out, for the kids are still small and my wife can't go out working.

So, she'll have to stay at home, and my income alone won't be enough. But since I don't go to Greece anyway, and the kids have to go to school so they can get ahead, so that human beings can be made out of them, who won't have to go around searching for work; we'll see. My wife is capable, but she'll have to get accustomed to Germany. I've calculated that I would need over ten thousand marks to bring everyone here, and with which we could move into an apartment.

W... 12.11.1971

Our beloved Father,

We're all doing fine, and hope that you're doing likewise. Can you believe it, Father, our goat, the hot-headed one, has calved two kids, and our Dimitrakis sits in front of them all day looking at them. I'm already grown-up now and when you come you won't recognize me; I'm in third grade now. Yesterday, I got another 10, and the teacher said, "Look what a good student Marigoula is." That's how he talked to the other kids. I just don't know why he calls me "Marigoula."
Every afternoon we go with Grandpa and Grandma to pick olives. "Thankfully," Grandma says, "Grandpa didn't come down with his rheumatism this year, and so he can load the bags onto the donkey." Dimitrakis comes along as well, but he's small and leaves half the olives behind him. Grandma scolds him; she says that

he should pay attention because the olives are drachmas, but Grandpa says, "Don't worry, I'll pick them up." Grandma is knitting a vest for you; she wants to send it to you, when somebody is heading your way. We, the children, think a lot about you and love you very much. Tomorrow is Saturday, and I'll bring flowers to Mom's grave. Dad, I'm asking you, let me to go to high school when I finish elementary school. Mom died because she got held back in the storm outside (in the field).

Hugs for you, Dimitrakis,
Grandpa and Grandma, and I

Strike II [3]

- Aren't you joining the strike?
    - No, not me.
- Why?
    - That's why. I want to work. I have three children.
- What are the strikers demanding?
    - 11% wage increase.
- Don't you want a raise?
    - I want one. But I have three children. They're in the village.
- Then why didn't you go into the factory, but hang around here in the street?
    - I'm afraid.
- Afraid of what?
    - They will taunt me in the evening. Do you know what they are?
    They can pummel you.
- Then go and join them.
    - That won't work, I've told you. My three children are in the village and I want to go down to see them. They have family here.

Kavala, 1981

Antonis K.

I went to Germany in 1962, when I was twenty-eights-years years old. I'd just been married for a year. After two years, and having discovered that money wasn't to be found on the street, my wife came as well; she is three years younger than I. We stayed until 1979 and then decided to return, as we had build-up a full fifteen-year pension period. Moreover, we couldn't stand it any longer to live far away from our

---

3 TN: There was a sharp increase in foreign workers' activism in the wake of the crashing halt to the German economic boom in the early 1970s.

children. When living in Germany we had two children, but we never had them live with us. You see, we both had to go out to work and we didn't have anyone to look after the kids. Then, there was also the apartment, we didn't have a suitable one for so many people, and we didn't find any other. So we decided to head back. We told each other, we would quickly raise the money to go back to our village. We had left them here in the village with my parents; they were going to school and we saw them for one month each year. But that wasn't a good move. We've been reunited for almost a year now and they haven't yet got used to us. They're closer to their grandfather and grandmother than with their own parents. That also breaks our hearts. Somehow we've established ourselves now; we bought our own house, and we have another one that we rent out, we brought furniture and electrical goods from Germany and I've a pretty decent job in a machine factory. And yet, we've not really settled in and sometimes I'm ashamed that I cannot do whatever the others do. We're used to doing things differently and Germany, how we talk, how we behave, and also about how we approach life. Many people find it odd that we go on an outing or don't work on Saturdays. Some friends here call us "the Germans" and I'm anxious that we'll never be able to fit back in completely, but what should we do, our home is here and we'll live here. The worst of all is what has happened to our children. One is twelve and the other nine. Both girls. They're going to school, and when I ask them how they're getting on in class they answer dryly: fine. And yet, they tell their grandfather how they spent the entire morning. They're not interested in the stories we tell them about Germany, while they tell each other their secrets and giggle. They don't seem to have confidence in us. As though they, too, speak of us as "Germans." It's seems they're still cross that we left them alone for so many years.

Dear Beloved Father Veysel Dağ

Dear beloved father,   31.11.1972

Before starting my letter I would like to extend my greetings to you and I yearningly kiss both of your hands in respect. Tell me, how are you, are you fine, I pray to God that you are fine and alright. If you want to ask how your son Veysel has been, thank God, I am doing well and healthy. Dear daddy, grandmother, Nana, and little Meryem came. Nana sends her greetings to you and kisses your eyes![1] Little Meryem sends her greetings and yearningly kisses your hands. Mom sends her greetings and holds your hands softly, carefully as if she was smelling a bouquet of roses. Cemile Hatun and Hasan, both send their greetings and yearningly and carefully kiss your hands. Uncle Süleyman and Aunt Anişe send their greetings and fondly hold your hands. Meryem, Perihan, Kasım, Mehmet, Hüseyin, Mustafa, they all send their greetings and kiss your hands. Once again I greet and kiss your hands. The sender, your son Veysel Dağ, waits for your prompt reply. I have received the letters you sent. We have bought a stove. Winter is almost upon us, once it snowed in the countryside, but it melted. What else is new over there at yours? The winter has arrived here now and there are storms. Tell us the news from there. Here, the stove has been set up already and everyone lights their stove. Dear daddy, bring me a cap gun. Last year you brought one for me, please bring another one like that. The day I wrote this letter, we were eating hedik.[2] My mother was eating hedik while I was writing this letter.
We wrote this letter on a Friday night. Children gathered around the brasier; on top of it, cauldron of hedik was being cooked. My mother said to Hasan: "Hey, whose son are you?", and Hasan said: "Close your eyes, all of you". Send us some money. We will buy a lamb for Eid. Send us some money, no matter how, but not less than 500.

Kestane kebap, gerisi sevap, acele cevap[3]
Shoe sizes: Veysel: 32, Cemile: 34, Mom: 37, Hasan: 21, Hatun: 27
The hand of your son, Veysel
Sender Veysel Dağ

---

1 Büyüklerin ellerinden, küçüklerin gözlerinden öpmek – kissing the hands of the elderly, kissing the eyes of the young (little persons) - terms of endearment

2 boiled wheat

3 "Chestnut kebap, eating it is good deed, quick reply" – literal translation. A tongue twister mostly written at the end of letters in order to indicate a wait for a response

Sayın çok kıymetli Babacığım
Satırlarıma başlamadan önce Sonsuz selamlar yolar-
Uzun bir ayrılık hasiretiyle her iki elerinden
doya doya öperim bakalım nasılsın iyi misin iyi ve
rahat olmanı ulu tanrıdan dilerim eğer sende oğlun
veyseli soracak olursan Hamd olsun canım sağ
ve sihalim yerindedir babacığım Ninem ile küçük meyrem
ile Geldiler ninem selam eder Gözlerinden doya doya
öper küçük meyrem selam eder elerinden doya doya
öper annem selam eder elerinden incitmeden
bir deste Gül Gibi kokulayarak elerinden sıkar
Cemile Hatun Hasan ayrı ayrı selam eder her iki
elerinden incitmeden doya doya öperler— suluyman amca
anişe teyze selam eder elerinden incitmeden sıkarlar
meyrem perihan kasım mehmet hüseyin mustafa
ayrı ayrı selam eder elerinden öperler
Tekrar selam eder elerinden öperim Gönderen
oğlun veysel Dağ acele cevap Beklerim
Göndermiş olduğun mektupları aldım
biz bir Fırınlı soba aldık burada Artık kış geliyor
köyde bir kerekar   Gön. veysel Dağ
yağıp kalkmış
orada havadisler nasıl burada
havadisler Artık kıştır burada Fırtanalar vardır

oradaki havadisleri bize bildir barada artık.
sobayı kurdular herkeş sobasını yakıyor.
Babacığım Bana bir Çatpatı Tabancası getir
Geçen sene bana birtane Getirmiştin aynı
onabenzer bir tabanca bana getir ▪▪▪
yazdığımızı gün hedik yiyorduk Annem
Gil hedik yiyordu bende yazıyordu bu mektubu
Cuma akşamı yazdık çocukları başına Birikmiş mar
nkalın ystunde bir kazan hedik ennem husme
dediki sen kimin oğlusun dedi Hasan dediki
hepiniz özünüzü örtür diyor
Bize Biraz Parasal biz kurban bayramında
kurBanlık alacağın nekadar salıyorsansal ama 500aşağı
inme
Kestane: Kebap Yimesi Bebap Acele cevap
Beklerim
                                  Ayakabıların numarası
                                  Veyselinki 32 Cemile
                                  35 - Annem 37 -
                                  Hasan 21 - Hatun
                                  27

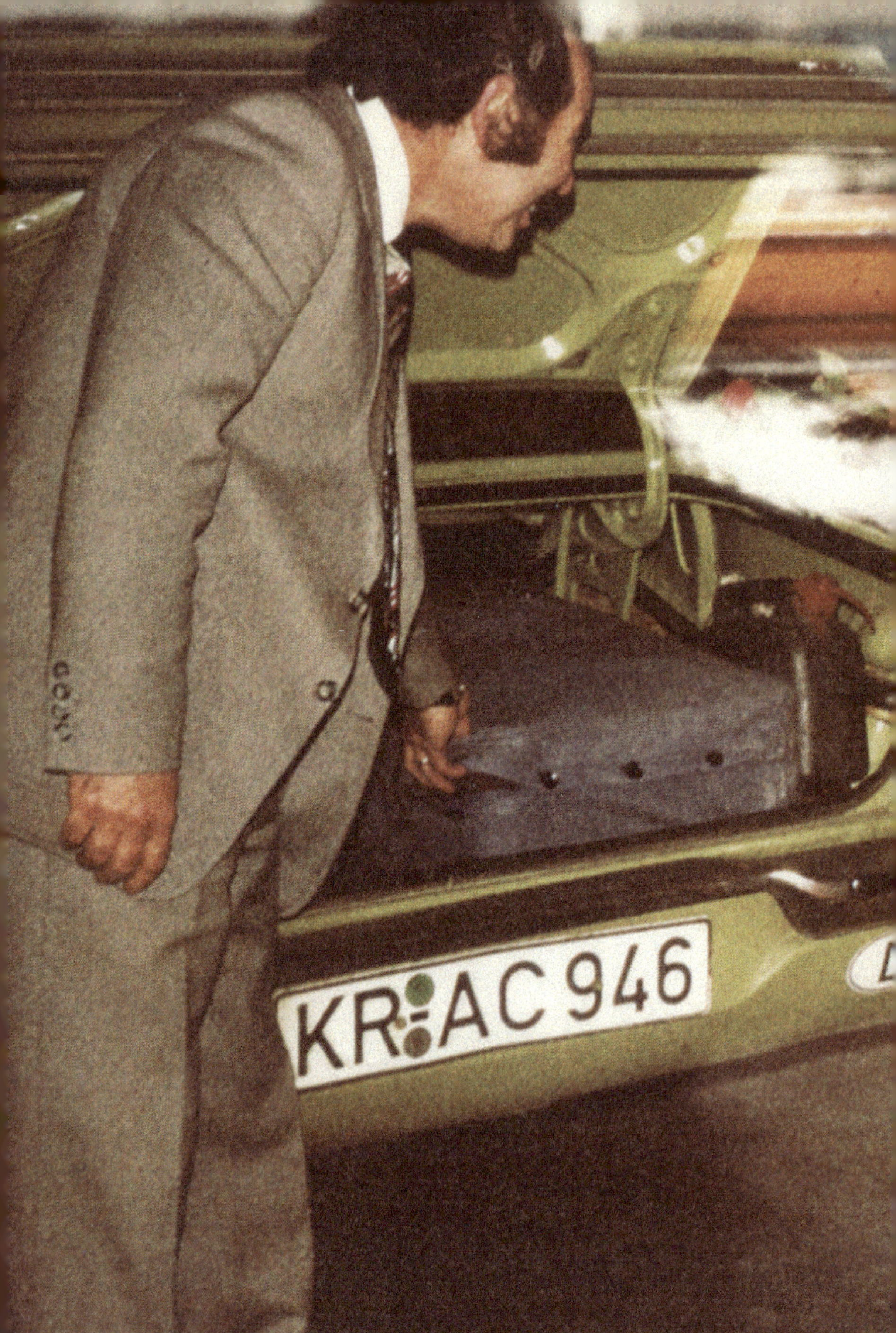

KR AC 946

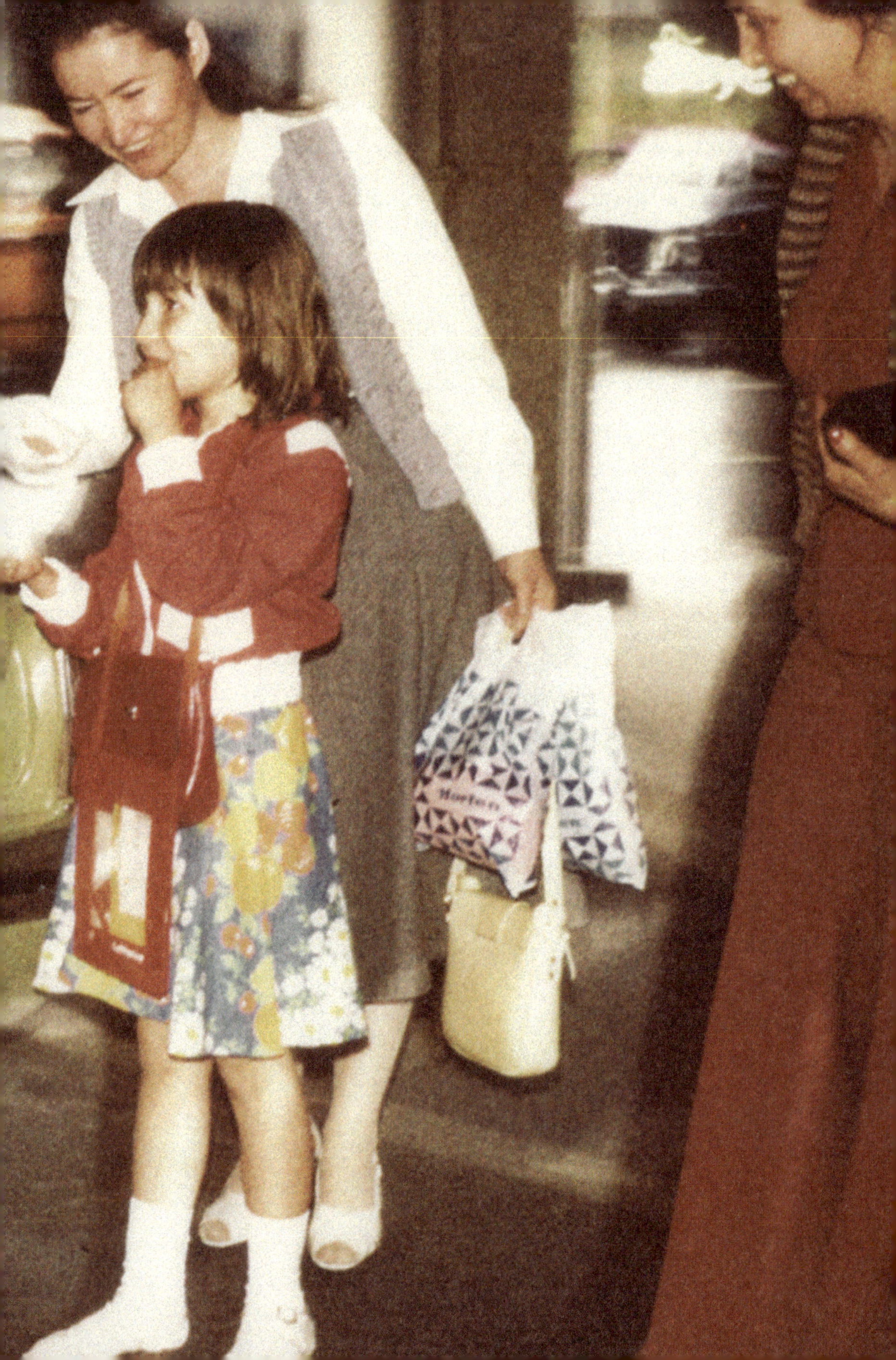

In his autobiographical story *Milk in Paper* (2011), the author Stefano
Polis reflects on his childhood as a 'suitcase child', to-ing and fro-ing
between Greece and Germany in the 1970s. Like many other children
of migrant workers, Polis grew up with an aunt after his parents had
emigrated. 'Guest workers' who wanted to bring with their families with
them to Germany first had to prove to the authorities that they could
provide adequate accommodation. This often considerably delayed the
process of family reunion.

Milk in Paper

Stefano Polis

The door was wide open that day, and music came from my father's old tape recorder. It was the voice of Kazantzidis, the Greek folk-singer, who sang about the "cursed foreign land." In his song, he sang about those people who either intend to leave their homeland – for whatever reason – or those who have been living abroad for a long time, far from home and their families.

His lyrics were simple and understandable to everyone, but at that time I couldn't thread the links between these lyrics and my own family circumstances. I listened to this song innocently and laughed, albeit in a very subdued way. I hid the nascent desire to find out why so many people had gathered in our house. In the hallway, a few elderly gentlemen were sitting around some suitcases, trying to distract themselves from their sadness with trivial conversation. Their talking, however, had only but one issue, usually ending with the word *Xenitiá*, the Greek for "foreign land." A word like a stony path that one has to walk barefoot. How many times had I heard that word over the last few days and never gave it a second thought.

Everywhere in the house were faces that I could only identify with difficulty. God, so many people – I'd almost forgotten that. Obviously an exceptional day. With feeble, subdued voices they bade each other courage. On the way to the kitchen I noticed the bedstead in the bedroom. Someone had removed the mattress and the bed stood there as though forgotten. When I was afraid at night, which happened regularly, my mother brought me to this bed. She then told me stories of better times in a more beautiful world. A world in which men love and respect their wives, take care of their families, love their children, and lie in bed with their wife at night.

Moreover the kitchen was unlike what it had been in the previous days. Dishes were nowhere to be seen and our small table was missing. Only faint shadows suggested that pictures once hung on those grey walls, and there, where yesterday the sofa sat, was nothing. Helplessly lost for words, I realized that something irresistible was forcing me out of my world. I ventured to wander through the empty house, bumping into women who were crowding around my mother, and silent men blankly staring into space. We Greeks like to chasten ourselves. It is an ancient custom to strive to improve our lot in every situation. –"You'll see, a year passes in no time," said one of the women to my mother."What's in a year, you know Sofia Krinou, she's been in Germany for a year, too. She's doing very well there and has picked up the language as well."

But no phrase, no matter how lovingly spoken, could reassure my mother, not in the slightest. Slumped in the arms of my aunt Irini, she wept incessantly.

"Dora, listen to me," I heard my aunt Lina say in a melodious voice, and that somehow gave me strength. But her next sentence was to shatter everything: "The children will be fine with me, I promise you. They'll want for nothing." "You magician, you thief, you *Xenitiá*" Kazantzidis calls the foreign land in his songs. He insists that the *Xenitiá*, the foreign land, only summons the best people, and he implores it to return these people soon. His songs are similar to trains people take on unknown journeys. Journeys on which worlds await discovery and a lot stands to be relinquished. Eventually, someone had to distract me after I kept asking about my mother, expressing the wish to stay at her side; I was dismissed with hypocritical explanations."You don't have to explain much to a child," I heard a woman say. "Children don't understand that," said another. "And besides, children forget quickly." [...]

The afternoon was coming to a close. The tension had eased off noticeably. Nobody dared utter lofty words or even make promises they knew they wouldn't fulfil. *Xenitiá*, *Xenitiá* were the conspicuous words ringing out of my father's cassette tape. *Xenitiá*. [...]

As my mother got into the taxi, our eyes crossed one last time through the crowd. For one brief moment, one last image of her that must have changed me forever. A tear-stained, pale face, with two eyes screaming for help as though in slow motion, stared at me. The taxi honked one last time and drove off. I couldn't get it into my head why my hitherto not so cosy world suddenly was torn asunder. My fear was replaced by anger and I really felt like insulting my mother. Yes, I wanted to insult her with any word I could think of. It never dawned on me that she really had no other choice. My childlike mind couldn't grasp what kind of trade-off she had entered into so as to give us children a better life.

"Have a good trip!" called out the crowd surrounding my aunt and I, to my mother, even from a distance. Hands were waving high above their heads like quivering flags, symbols of an episode about to come to an end. I stood there, speechless, and my earlier anger gradually subsided. For the first time I now felt this paralyzing emptiness in me. That emptiness that took hold of me thereafter and grimly grips me as soon as I stretch out my hand to bid someone farewell. [...]

A letter from my mother that we received two years later comes to mind. My aunt had first read it on that morning. Then, with a smile and teary-eyed, she looked at us and announced that my mother had given birth. Taken aback, I mentally searched for a face for the new-born. "It's a boy and his name is Georg, after our father," my aunt exclaimed, delighted.

I didn't know what kind of feelings I should choose. I had decided to distance myself from my parents, but in the face of such news, I was beset by grave doubts. The birth of my brother threw my hard-won ideal world off course. How should I deal with it and, above all, what feelings did I want to entertain? Every feeling I entertained posed a risk. A fascinating journey with an unknown destination. After hesitating at length, my imagination painted my brother's image. There, we were playing together and sharing many adventures. There, I called him by his name and he me by mine, and such thoughts rapidly took hold of me.

She also wrote that my father would fetch us in the summertime and we would then be a real family at long last. Confused, I constantly asked myself only the one question: A real family, what was that supposed to be? Wasn't I living in a real family, even though it wasn't my own, and why should I jeopardize the love of this family? The more I thought about it, the more confused my thoughts became, and every shred of curiosity about the new country, about my mother and my brother that were awakening in me, were nipped in the bud. In the hope that my parents' plans would come to nothing, I tried blocking out all thoughts on this matter.

Nevertheless, my apprehensions materialised quicker than I would have preferred. One fine morning, an unfamiliar car stopped in front of our door and a tall man in a suit got out. Laughing, he paid his fare and bade goodbye to the driver. His searching look through the iron gate revealed a longing. He was wearing a hat like those worn by gentlemen in black-and-white films and was carrying two suitcases. Two sightly whiskers almost reached his chin. His suit fitted him like a glove and his shoes were freshly polished.

"Lina, Lina, where are you?" were his first words, at the top of his voice.

My dumbfounded aunt emerged from around the corner. Drying her hands on her apron, she sought out the strange man. She stopped in front of the iron gate. Passing her hands through her hair and then over her rosy face, a tight smile played on her lips. Her eyes opened widely.

"Philip, my brother-in-law, where have you come out of?" My heart pounded on hearing the man's name. As white as a sheet, I hid myself in the stairwell to the bread cellar and wanted to be left alone by everyone. I can't recapitulate any longer what was going through my head. In the seclusion of the stairwell I saw how my problem could be solved. From my hiding place I reluctantly listened to the voices of all those partaking in the welcoming reception. They greeted each other and cried. Like mist early in the morning, a mood was unfolding that terrified me, and I looked around for my little sister. In the midst of my agitation I had overlooked that she had followed me and was now sitting next to me. She was crouching on her knees and grinning like a Cheshire cat. She was wrapping her lower lip with her tongue. "Shall we play hide-and-seek, Stefo?" she asked. [...] I was still scared and wanted – if only I could! – to erase this moment from my consciousness. I felt queasy and cold to boot.

Today, I recall the discomfort that such situations triggered in me over the following years – until this very day. A mixture of nausea and frenzy, and whenever I closed my eyes in despair – in the belief that I was eluding it – I found myself in a dark room with long curtains hanging from the ceiling that blocked me from moving forward. As though paralyzed, I plodded around between the long curtains in search of the exit.

"Koulitza, your Dad's here, come out, he's brought you loads of things. And a doll, as well." For a moment, my sister's little eyes opened widely. Her lips formed a smile. "Did you hear that? I'm going, come with me," she decided instantly. I thought, oh God, why does this have to happen? I hated such moments and wished it were all over.

My sister really meant it. She really wanted to head upstairs. That meant I would be left all alone down there in the stairwell. Perhaps then I would have to leave my hiding place by myself and that would even be harder for me. Nothing could be done about it; I had to get it over with and greet him, and the sooner the better. After a short prayer I crossed myself three times; then I was ready. Like a programmed robot, I stood up and took my sister by the hand. What was there to it, there were only a thousand steps to a hell that was unfolding on our patio at that moment, and yet another thousand steps to my father. Every single step on this endless path was agonizing, and the closer we got, the larger the lump in my throat grow. All attempts to swallow it failed. My senses, in turn, switched off. I decided not to look at him and let everything pass through me, and not utter a sound anyway – as I'd always done in such situations since my mother's leave-taking.

I almost fainted as we reached our target, my heart beating so loud that every one could hear it. Smiling faces and a chorus of voices surrounded us. Hereafter everything seemed to go out of control in me. No organ in my body obeyed me. The world around me turned to slow motion.

Real and unreal worlds fused in such a way that I could only perceive segments. In this trance-like state, I was hugged and greeted. Then I was able to sit on a chair until such time as I woke out of it.

A few minutes passed before I awoke from the 'narcosis', and could once again distinguish voices and had to answer countless questions until my aunt Lina rescued the situation by asking our father whether he was hungry. He said yes, whereupon aunt Lina set up the garden table in a makeshift manner. Evangeli diligently brought bread and cheese. Aunt Lina expertly transformed the ripe tomatoes and cucumbers, which uncle Kostas had promptly brought from the garden, into a colourful salad. The table was covered in a jiffy with everything that is tasty and filling. My aunt forgot nothing. I, however, sat as though I had taken root in the chair and only slowly came around. "Come, brother-in-law, don't be embarrassed and help yourself," she urged him on. Our father didn't need any further encouragement. While he was cutting bread, aunt Lina recited "Our Father." With the exception of my father, everybody reverently made the sign of the cross. My hands were tied and Koulitza had other ideas – the new doll demanded her full attention.

While he was eating, I observed him very closely. A strange man, who at once aroused in me uncertainty and deep interest. When we used to live together, much to my mother's and my chagrin, he was very rarely at home, and whenever he happened to be there he hardly spoke to us. Whenever in his company, one couldn't help but feel that his thoughts were always elsewhere. He never liked answering questions, and he seldom asked any. Every encounter with him was always accompanied by fear, which I can no longer explain. Perhaps due to the fact that he could get so insistent about every trifle or that he didn't treat my mother very well. He was only happy whenever he could hang out with his friends. Preferably at a *kafenio*, where he would play backgammon enthusiastically. His presence left us in no doubt whatsoever that he would take us both with him.

I didn't want to go to Germany, that was for sure. I swore to myself that I wouldn't leave my homeland. No way would I back down. Nothing could persuade me. Not even the sight of the suitcase, which stood on the steps of the house, beckoning me. Out of the blue my father asked, "Have you been taking good care of your sister, Stefanaki?" as he dabbed the salad plate with a piece of bread. I wasn't ready for that question. I first took a swallow. Immediately afterwards I lowered my head and felt like a pupil being questioned by his teacher.

"Yes," I said meekly. "Were you a good boy as well?" Another anxious "yes" ensued. He leaned back, stroking his face. At the same time I noticed his smile – it took away my tremendous fear.

"Do you two want to come to Germany with me?" I shrugged my shoulders, not wanting to give too much of my feelings away. Bewildered, I pretended to be obliging. But deep inside of me, I was seeking a resolution. "Open that little suitcase," my father interrupted my thoughts. My sister, less hesitantly, stood in front of the suitcase with her new doll under her arm and tried to open it. Without a doubt, she must have got the doll while I was under "narcosis." My father nodded suggestively. "Come on, Stefanaki, help her." I was curious about the suitcase, but was still reluctant to approach it. After a few minutes and a bit more coaxing by my aunt, the tenseness dissolved in me, and I took advantage of my father's brief inattention to approach the suitcase. My sister greeted my decision with a smile, and together we opened the suitcase and were overwhelmed by the grandiose contents. Through their sheer presence, countless bags of sweets, lots of chocolate and many colourful bars quenched our hunger for sweet things. I had never seen so many beautiful things at one time. My initial hesitation subsided, and I was just waiting to be prompted to taste these glorious delights.

"That's all for you, you can help yourselves to anything." That had to be the starting signal. With pleasure we attacked the sweets and tried one bar at a time. While soft chocolate melted throughout my mouth, a number of thoughts went through my head. This Germany might indeed be interesting, and the longing to see my brother grew steadily. This change of mind was without a doubt triggered in part by the many things that had descended upon us like a godsend.

"There's more of the same in Germany," my father said. Suddenly, this country struck me as more and more likeable. If I had one of these bars every day, then I might well change my mind and go with him, I thought. "They have the best things there, I tell you. There's nothing that cannot be found there."

"Are there animals in Germany?" I asked, wondering about myself. Courage was not my strong point, but chocolate could loosen my tongue. "Oh yes, quite a lot." My father told us a few things about that foreign country. About his experiences in Germany, which were only the best. About the people there, the houses, the streets, the landscape. And then he started talking about my mother and brother and somehow my initial timidity faded and I felt a great desire to learn more about them. I dared to ask more questions, all those that interested me the most then. So I asked my father: "Are there cows as well?" After my father had confirmed to me that there were lots of cows in Germany, my thirst for knowledge increased rapidly and I decided to ask about my favourite drink. "And milk, what about milk?" He laughed, finishing the last sip from his glass. Then he turned again to my sister and I, looking at us seriously. "There's milk as well, and you won't believe it, it's packed into paper bags." All our faces displayed silent amazement. "Milk in paper? How do they do that?" my aunt asked in disbelief. At that very moment, the desire to learn more about this milk in paper sprouted in me. A curious idea aroused suspicion in me that Germans must be able to perform magic. Yes, I wanted to see this milk in paper, at all costs.

Following Italy, Spain, Greece, Turkey, and Morocco, the Federal Republic of Germany concluded a labour recruitment agreement with the Republic of South Korea in December 1963. From 1963 until recruitment stopped in 1977, some 8000 Korean mine workers came to work in West Germany. As of 1966, around 11000 South Korean nurses followed them. Torn between the yearning for parental love and the joy of receiving gift packages from Germany, Ok-Hee Jeong encapsulates the perspective of a child left behind.

My Parents live in Germany

Ok-Hee Jeong

My little hands eagerly unpack a glittering red-green gift package. This morning someone from the city brought a large package for my Grandma. Many colourful stamps, below right – the neatly written address of our house, diagonally top left in untidy handwriting my parents address in a country that is called Germany. My aunts explain that there are two Germanys; one is called West Germany and the other East Germany. Just like with us in Korea. Only here we call them South and North Korea. West Germany, my parents live there.

Mom and Dad have placed a small gift-box for each of us inside the large package. Honey and jam for Grandma, as well as medicine for her pains; for my aunts lots of little make-up jars with pastel-collared powders and silky creams; for my two brothers toy cars and plastic bricks that they can assemble. And my gift-box? I carefully open my present so as not to rip the fancy paper apart. I hold a pair of shoes in my hands. Green-blue, shiny shoes, the leather feels cloud-like soft, with thick, solid, black soles. I try them on immediately. They feel very heavy and clunky on my feet, which are more accustomed to light rubber shoes. A pity … for they're far too big … Of course, Mom no longer knows how big I am. She hasn't seen me for three years. Blue and green, too bad … my favourite colours are pink and yellow.… But still, I jump around the house with shoes that are too big and I could fly with joy, for my Mom and Dad had been thinking of me, and hadn't forgotten me, and sent such an expensive gift from a country so far away. Grandma urges me to go outdoors with my new shoes, but I'd better take them off so that they don't get dirty. I embrace her tightly in my arms and run outside to join my friends, out into the village alleys. "Nara-ya, Sunhi-ya, look what my parents have sent me from Germany!" The next day, I cautiously and proudly take the silver-collared pencil sharpener from Germany out of my school bag and lay it carefully next to my copybook. Immediately word spread among the fifty or so students in the class: "Mira got a pencil sharpener from Germany!"

During class break, a crowd forms around my desk. "Let me, will you?

It's my turn now, right? Hey, come on, let me have a go!" So much attention makes me very embarrassed, but somehow proud and happy as well. But what a misfortune, by the end of the day the sharpener has been stolen! On packing my schoolbag after class, I'm missing the silver-coloured sharpener. No matter how many tears I shed, they won't bring it back. Don't they know it's a gift from my Mom? My belly hurts so much, as though my Mom had been stolen from me.

But, actually three years ago Germany stole my Mom and Dad away from me. My mother works as a nurse for the Germans. My father works as a miner for the Germans. "You'll have to be very good, and always listen carefully to Grandma and to your aunties. When we return, Dad and Mom will bring back so much money and lots of presents from Germany. But always be good to Grandma and your aunts, do you hear!" At the airport, my aunts were crying, and even Grandma, who otherwise was so tough, shed a few tears, and there I stood at the age of five, laughing aloud, for I didn't know why I should be sad, for Mom had promised to come back soon and bring us many presents, and besides it had to be wonderful and exciting to fly by plane, and I waved eagerly with my weeping three-year-old brother holding my hand while tracing the plane's path, without noticing that the sun had silently been ripped out my belly and had disappeared by plane, way, way beyond the horizon, for a long, a very long time.

My three-year-old brother cried all the way home from the airport. He couldn't be consoled. And from that day on, he demanded his mother's breast, even though he had long since stopped breastfeeding. Desperately, he looked for Grandma's breast so as to satisfy his longing for our mother. But after years of uninterrupted breastfeeding of her seven children, grandmother's breasts had long since dried up and hung soft, limp, and emaciated on her body, so that she could only take him clumsily in her arms to comfort him, and explained time and again that she was too old and that her breasts could no longer give him milk. And yet, nothing could comfort my brother. During the day he begged, crying for my grandmother's dried breasts and at night he wet himself in bed beside her. As of that day, something in his heart has been broken.

Slowly, the smile was also stolen from my face and in my belly I felt a cold, black hole crushing my tiny heart with its icy claws, whenever I was missing my Mom. And I missed her so much. It was ever so strange, for I knew I had a mother, and yet I didn't have a mother at the same time. That's how children without parents must feel, for I felt like an orphan somehow. But my parents aren't dead! Whenever we had a daytrip in the kindergarten and later at school, the other children came with their parents or with their mothers, holding their hands, jumping up beside them, laughing and talking at the top of their voices. My little hand just kept holding onto the hand of my wrinkled and strict Grandma, dressed in the traditional *Hanbok*, and I was ashamed amidst the children with their beautiful, young mothers, all prettily spruced up. I would have liked to run away or shout in everyone's face: "That's not really my mother, my real mother lives in well-to-do Germany and earns lots of money and anyway, my Mom is gorgeous, she is the most beautiful woman in the world and she is much prettier than your mothers! "

And whenever my grandma or my aunts scolded me, I secretly thought if Mom were there, then you definitely wouldn't dare do that. And sometimes, so many times, I just missed her so – her beautiful, bright voice, her warm, soft hands caressing my head, her smell and the warmth I felt as I lay in her arms ... just like that ... if only I could conjure her up.

If only...

My heart is throbbing wildly. Tomorrow I will fly for the first time ever. On a plane. To Germany. To my parents. Finally. Finally I can meet Mom and Dad again. On the eve of the trip, my uncle's wife takes me aside. "Are you looking forward to Germany?"

"Mm."

"Won't you be afraid in a foreign country?"
I shake my head. Why should I? Aren't my parents there and they will protect me from everything if danger ever threatens, or, so I secretly think.

"Aren't you going to miss us terribly?"

"Mm ..."

" Wouldn't you rather stay behind in Korea?" My heart is throbbing wildly. "You know that I've only two sons. Don't you want to stay with me forever? To be my daughter forever? " I sit there, heart fluttering, not knowing what to say. I just scent danger. One false word and I'll have to stay here forever and be forever separated from my true mother. Why does my aunt keep asking such strange things, doesn't she know that I already have a mother? Doesn't she know that it just seemed as though I didn't have one? I keep looking at the ground. It strikes me that with a single word it will be decided, whether I'll be allowed see my mother again or not. A false word, a false look, a false move, and I'll have to stay with my aunt forever. "Just don't look at her! Don't you hear? Don't look at her! If you look, you're lost," a voice whispers nervously. Without looking up, I firmly shake my head, at first silently and softly, but then trembling and boldly.

Finally.

Finally the time has come. We children are dressed in our best new clothes. I'm wearing a beautiful red dress and feel like a princess. And in no time we're sitting in the plane, so much bigger than anything I've ever seen before. The flight to Germany takes us half way round the world. My older brother says: "You know, if we fly over Russia, we'll arrive much, much faster in Germany. But then the communists will shoot us down with a missile. That's why we're flying in the opposite direction, over where the Americans live and they're our friends."

Only that way takes a lot, lot longer. Sleep once more, and then I'll finally see my parents again. When I wake up, we're nowhere near Germany, but it is midnight and we're in a strange country. Alaska. Anchorage. I'm in an icy world, where polar bears and Eskimos supposedly live.

Carefully and intently, I look out into the darkness to catch a glimpse of the polar bear that my older brother had told me about. Instead of a polar bear I only catch sight in the glass panel of a delicate young girl in a red dress with two thick plaited waist-length braids, standing in the middle of the huge and strangely silent airport hall in glaring neon lights. It looks like thousands of grey ice crystals are enveloping them. The feathery snowflakes keep falling and falling from the great dark hole of the sky. In the background I can see some adults dozing, separately, in empty rows of chairs, as is Grandma in her *Hanbok*. My heart is still throbbing excitedly. The hall is cool, but still it feels so nice and warm in my belly. Oh, just one more sleep, and then I'll see my kingly parents again. For I imagine that my parents are wearing royal robes and dwell in a castle, and I will soon be a princess.

Frankfurt Airport, Germany.

A strange woman is clutching me in her arms. This woman, who looks haggard and exhausted, is not my Mom at all, and not even a queen, that I had been remembering for three years. Instead of calling her Mom, I bow deeply, as I had been taught in Korea, that one ought bow to adults, eyes to the ground, and mumble: "*Annyoung hasaeyo* - how are you?"

The woman holds me tightly in her arms, and with tears of joy she keeps pressing her cold lips on my cheeks over and again. I want to tear myself away from her embrace, but just stand there stiffly and redfaced. I really want to ask my grandmother: And, what if all this is not true? Maybe they're not my parents at all and they're just pretending? And it's all just one terrible mistake? I watch my grandmother's every single movement and facial expression. Grandma is laughing. Grandma is crying. Grandma is laughing. Grandma would hardly fall for a trick, would she? Might they be my real parents after all? My thoughts surge excitedly as I hastily seek out my brother's eyes, asking and begging; but they're all laughing, while Grandma laughs and cries, the strange man laughs and keeps calling out our names, and the strange woman? Slowly, my heart turns pleasantly sad, pleasantly happy, pleasantly quiet while my heartbeat slowly fades from quiet to quieter, as I once again deeply recognize, yes, very deeply in my belly my dearest Mom. Yes ... that's how she always felt. Just like that.

Or?

According to a study by the International Organization for Migration (IOM), around 177,000 unaccompanied children live in Moldova, whose parents work abroad. Owing to the current economic predicament in Moldova, people emigrate to Russia, Western Europe, or Turkey. The Moldavan writer Liliana Corobca describes the fate of twelve-year-old Cristina, who takes care of her little brothers Dan and Marcel. Their father is in Russia, her grandmother is ill, and their mother is looking after the children of a wealthy family in Italy. Corobca recounts the children's everyday life from Cristina's perspective, where one understands that the situation demands of her that she becomes an adult before her time.

Kinderland

Liliana Corobca

How difficult are the days going by without you! [...]

One is crying, the other one wants something to eat and turns the kitchen upside down looking for the sugar bowl in the process. I gave them jam, but they complain they're getting tummy aches from eating jam on bread. I saw someone, poorer than us, putting bread slices under the running tap, then dipping the moist slices in coats of sugar. Since that day onwards, all the children ever want is sugar-coated bread slices though it angers me having to watch them dip their moist bread slices into the sugar pouch. It's enough for the older one to start crying for no good reason to get the younger one howling too as if that had him switched on. And they both howl relentlessly, much like a pair of wolf cubs abandoned in the woods. All they want though is have someone coddling them, making them feel as if they matter. I need that too, regardless of how much of a grown-up I may be. I want a mother by my side: cooking for me, washing my dresses. Ironing them too.

I told them: keep your hearts on your finger tips and blow them off hard until they fly all the way to reach mother. And she'll carress those spoon-fed children that get mango fruit to eat as if she'd carress us. Surely, you start crying too once you start thinking about us, don't you? And when you wash up those children's clothes – made up of natural wool, cotton or silk, most of which were given to you by the Italians you work for to send back to us after you've washed them up so many times that they no longer look new – you must be sparing a thought for our clothes too. If my brothers were to know that, they'd stop wearing them. They'd rather go without so many branded clothes, manufactured from natural fibres, if only they could have their mother back. Maybe those sweet and gentle children you are caring for are crying too because their mother left them in another woman's care. [...]

Stop crying, now we have work to do! We should have a schedule in place. Crying time: 8 o'clock in the evening. It's better this way. What if I were to start crying the minute you get hungry? Or when the chicken and the rest of the cattle have no water and are dying of thirst? As if your crying were the most important thing in the world...

When Marcel is on the verge of crying, I say to him: 'Come with me, please, let's beat the carpets, let's water the plants'. I find something for him to do and, after that, I tell him: 'You do this first and afterwards you can cry as much as you please.' This way he forgets about crying. Sometimes, though, he'd have none of it and would cry his head off regardless, waiting for me or Dan to come and comfort him alright. We feel for him yet, if we go near, we remind ourselves of mum and dad and we start crying all the same.

After telling him that we'll cry according to the timetable - how forgetful of me, hey? - one evening, Marcel brought with him, at eight o'clock sharp, no less, mum and dad's photos; he set them up before us just as a film was about to start and said: It's eight o'clock! It's crying time! Take those pictures back now!... we ranted. Can't you see the film is about to begin? Only fools and screaming infants cry! Real men toughen up and face up to adversity. The child had had enough listening to us so he left there and took the pictures with him too. I went 'round to see what he was up to and found him mumbling something untoward. He must've been complaining to the parents in those photos how cruel and brutish siblings he had since all they could think about was watching films rather than think about their parents [...].

I made a sock puppet by dressing a pillow up, put a kerchief over one of its corners and there was mum. You want mother, well, here's mother for you then. I slid my hand through one of the sleeves, and, in theatrical style, mother began pouring tea for her much-loved son. Dan played along. – Mummy, can I have some of that awesome tea, pretty please? Yet, Marcel began hitting the pillow making me to spill some of the hot tea in the pot. – I'll have no tea from a pillow! It ruined the mood entirely. We thought a bit of role-play would be fun and would enliven the atmosphere.

Next time you leave tell him that three days beforehand. Prepare him psychologically. Dan deals with it, he doesn't cry, I tell him how big a boy he is, like you said, he's the man in the household, soon enough he'll be going to school where he'll wear the nicest suit, carry around the most attractive backpack, have proper notebooks and writing materials, alas, everything he needs. This is why mother works hard, and father too, to make money, and everything they do is for our sake. I tell him that soon enough he'll be taller than me, that he is wise, mature, and can deal with the situation. [...]

Mother sends us no toys, nor does father. We get food money, clothes we need, made up of natural fibres, wool or cotton, bought second hand or left over from the children she's working for, some sweets too. We are to avoid becoming obese, because that affliction has no dietary remedy and children that grow fat get two or three additional illnesses also. Yet, other children get nice, expensive clothes; they turn up at the playground dressed in them and, in a matter of days, they turn them into rags, fit for the cattle. A boy in my classroom got a mobile phone from his dad. We were all watching him out of the corner of our eyes as he was listening to music during breaks and also writing messages during classes. The other boys were envious of him, they asked him to have a look at his phone, which duly slipped their clumsy hands, by mistake, a few times until it broke down for good.

Last year, mother brought me a princess' dress for the New Year's Eve concert party. I was so beautiful, like a queen amongst underlings and other mere mortals. They chose me as Queen of the ball, everyone had been fawning about how beautiful the dress was and I had been twirling around and dancing all evening. Only when I got back home I was able to see that it had been filled with holes made up by burning matches. I felt nothing, I had no idea as to whom might have been responsible for burning holes into my dress. There had been only smiling, admiring faces around me.

Mother was scared stiff that the dress could have gone up in flames and I could have ended up badly injured. She informed my tutor about what had happened, but the tutor was all at sea as the ball had been attended by everyone in the school and by children from the surrounding villages, we played up and bumped into each other – there was no way she could assert responsibility for what had happened. From that day onward, mother never bought me any fancy clothes that might set me apart. [...]

Expectation is like a small animal – neither domesticated nor wild, sometimes well behaved and sleepy, at other times evil and unleashed, walking before rationality and comforting thoughts. The waiting will be over soon. This time sequence becomes hard to endure, carry around with you, suffer. So hard that it pulls us down to the ground, getting us stooped by the burden of longing. Not even mother can bring herself to understand such a thing. As for myself, however, seeing my brothers look over our parents' photos makes me feel as if my belly were filled by a tonne of tears and were I to release them they'd engulf the entire village.

My way of waiting around is like a huge bunch of flowers, larger than myself, fragrant and vividly coloured, picked from all the surrounding hills, that you bring mother even though mother's not home. You come in and shout out: Mother! No one answers your call. Wildflowers tossed around the house, unto the clean and freshly swept *Ungheni* carpets. But a tender and equally resigned type of waiting alright.

Dan's way of waiting around resembles a bouncy ball that had visited every darkened corner, had quashed the vegetables in the neighbours' garden, and had been caught by a dog unable to sink its teeth into it. This is the type of youthful waiting that never gives up or grows tired. This is one angry type of waiting most impatient at that.

Marcel's way of waiting around resembles the boiling over of milk, flowing over the sides of the pot and unto the hob. As a pack of black clouds gathering out of nowhere to cover the entire sky before it starts pouring down. It's like an invasion of starlings over the wheat fields, or locusts devouring everything in their wake. His is a hungry and categorical type of waiting around, leaving you with no right of appeal whatsoever.

Our way of waiting around resembles a smouldering disease, an insistent virus that only goes away when parents are nearby. Dan's cough and fever were over as soon as mother came home. I was afraid that it might be contagious but then both Marcel and I were fine in the end. It is enough to have the parents back home and every illness gets instantly cured. Waiting around – like rain after drought. We are but shrivelled children, dried out by too much longing. Like a dried-out river bed. We're aged by having to wait around in the guise of responsible and mature people and we only get to regain our childhood once mother gets back home.

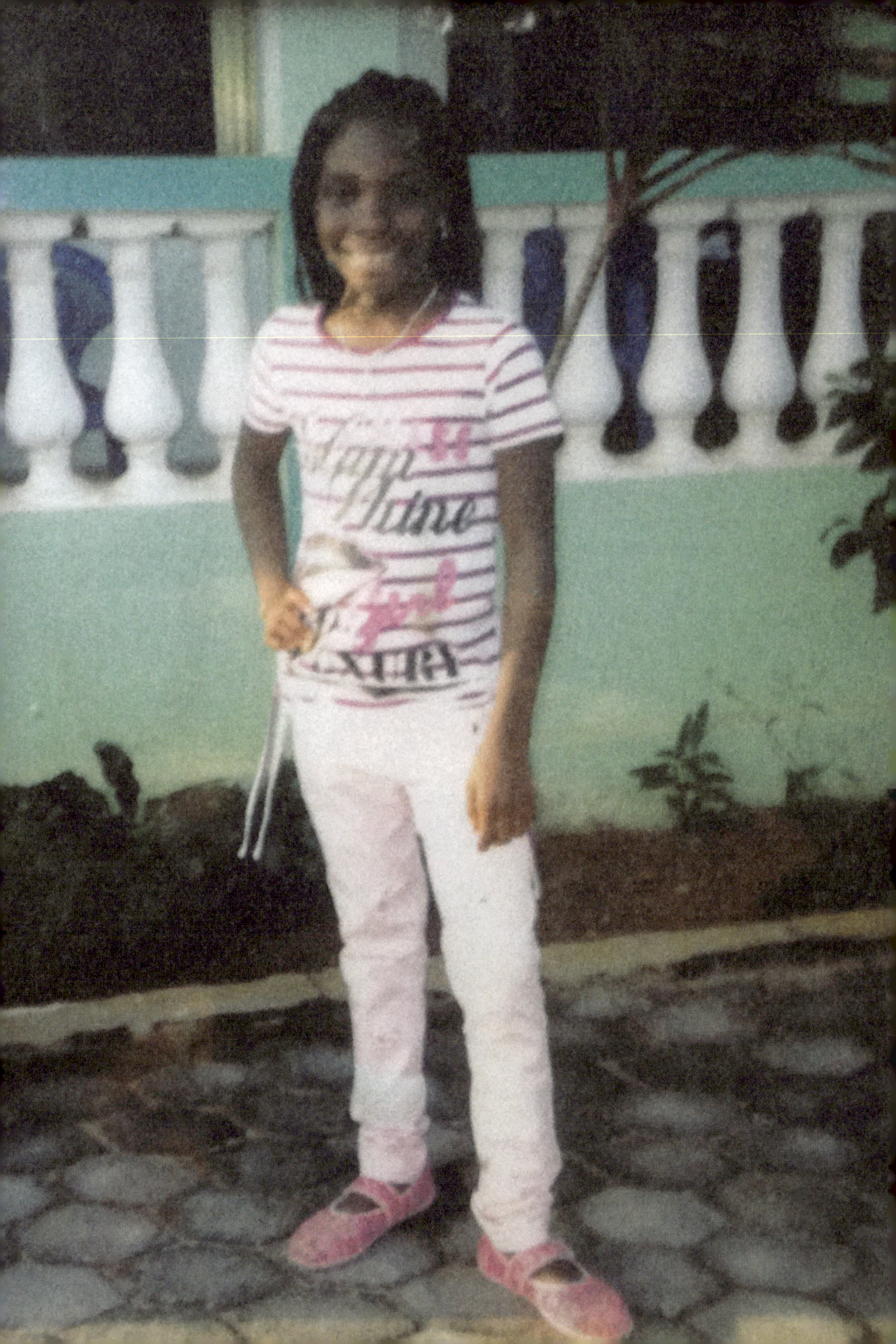

Halyna Kruk's short story *Ho Paura*[1] appeared in the anthology *Skype Mama* (2013), edited by Kati Brunner, Marjana Sawka, and Sofia Onufriv. *Skype Mama* features contemporary narratives from Ukraine, which deal with torn families through labour migration. The number of such families, in which one or both parents work abroad, is said to be in the millions in Ukraine. Communication via Skype is central in the relationship between mothers and children in the stories.

1 Italian: I'm afraid

Ho Paura

Halyna Kruk

"Lately Petro Titschyn said you'll never come back," Iwasyk said as though off-hand. The connection was poor, the end of the sentence grinding like a broken cassette tape.

"That's not true, Iwasyk," Nelja rapidly intercepted, how is this Petro supposed to know that, but the transmission was delayed, Skype was indicating that the speakers were not functioning properly.

"... like his Wasylyna. She remarried and got herself new children, and she doesn't care about the others anymore," whispered Iwas meanwhile at the other end. "You've got to speak in short sentences, otherwise I won't hear you!," she shouted again, but suddenly it went quiet. Perhaps the line was still intact, but perhaps not. She had to talk with her son, for she had already waited several days, but the message flashed on the screen:

The call is over. Duration: 3:27.

He sent her one of the many smileys, the one that squirms and explodes with anger, that is easier for him than a text message, for he had just got the computer and was typing with only one finger, and it took him a while to find the right letter. The smileys were like a new game to him, he wanted to test them all. Nelja wasn't keen on this gimmick, for how was she to know which face he was hiding behind and how he was really getting along.

Nelja clicked on the green handset again and asked several times:

"Do you hear me, Iwasyk? Is it better now?" The network in their area was bad, the connection unstable, that even telephone calls were interrupted over and again, and video connections were hopeless. But perhaps it wasn't because of the connection, but Iwasyk somehow got offended with her and simply didn't want to reply anything? "I'm here, I hear you, speak up," suddenly his voice got through to her from a distance.

"Of course, I'll come back, Iwasyk, you know that. But it'll take a little while, first we must pay off the loan for the apartment. And don't listen to Petro." "I've just smashed his face in, just to make sure that he doesn't compare you to Wasylyna, the old slut," Iwasyk replied. "You mustn't do such things, and how you talk, such language," Nelja objected hesitantly, but it sounded uncertain, as though she were afraid that her son might think she, too, was like Wasylyna. From the one side, he was still a child, and yet, he sometimes had something completely un-childlike, spiny and prickly in him. Like a hedgehog. "What do you want?" she reproached herself, "he's on his own, he must get along somehow, get through. You're far away, how have you any right whatsoever to educate him, you just patch up all the sharp corners during talk, so that the relationship doesn't break off."

"You're doing everything wonderfully, Iwasyk, you're so independent," she said aloud, as thought they were emerging from her own thoughts. "And what's Grandma up to?" "She keeps nagging. Her blood pressure is acting up, and something is constantly wrong with her." Her mother often really griped about that Iwas was sitting too long in front of the computer. That all his nonsense was gradually going way above her head. That she couldn't get her way with him any longer because he was stronger. Her mother was always a strong-willed woman, managing everything and finding a solution for everything. All she lacked was delicacy of feeling. Nelja would have always wanted that her mother just hug her, but she had always fended her off, with an "oh what, you with your beefy caresses always." That was exactly how she put it: beefy caresses. But wasn't that cute! Nelja had once seen how a cow licked her little new-born bull, a shaggy thing with trembling legs that were constantly giving way. She fancied Iwasyk as a small bull. Her son's photo in her purse was long out of date, but it was her favourite photo of him when he was about three and had fallen asleep in the bus, but they had to get out of it. At that time, as Nelja recalled, he rubbed his eyes with his tiny fists and, shortly after waking up, looked as sweet and rosy as a fresh bun.

"Have you food in? Is there enough?" Nelja asked, as always. "We've enough, I'm even going out to market myself and buy meat, for I already know my way around. Sometimes the market gets too much for Grandma," Iwas said proudly. "And how are things at school? Can you manage everything?" "Yes, I can cope, but I'm constantly at all the homework. Our teacher said that we should all donate money for plastic windows. "Your mother is in Italy after all, you have the money," she said.

"If I get my wages this month, I'll send you something right away," Nelja said, boiling with rage. Iwasyk's teacher knew exactly what the money was meant for: The loan for the apartment had to be paid off, and there wasn't much left over. Nelja tried to save wherever she could: At the supermarket, she chose food, whose sell-by-date had already expired; she bought clothes only during the sales. That's what all the guest workers were doing here. Yet, Nelja usually kept to her herself, she didn't like the gossiping. It was normal among women: one poured her heart out, while the second passed the word around, the third invented something out of jealousy, the fourth told it at home, and in the end something came out of it as happened to Wasylyna: In her case, someone had seen her arm in arm with an Italian man, and she was straightaway a slut.

And all because of that damn money that had driven her so far from home. Not greed, but poverty had driven her away. In the beginning she had worked for an old woman who was afraid of being robbed. There wasn't much to take, and all the cabinets, including the kitchen cupboard, were under lock and key. The old woman was so stingy that she wouldn't even treat herself to a slice of tart, but always came to the kitchen whenever Nelja was eating, so that Nelja would offer her something.

Iwasyk was worried about money, was that normal? When she was nine, she just got a few kopeks to go fetch bread or milk. With such comparisons Iwasyk always came out badly. She had had a typical Soviet childhood. Perhaps her parents had taken too much care of her and controlled her every step, but there had also been many beautiful things: In winter, her parents went ice-skating with her, in summer they took to the riverbanks, to pick mushrooms or berries. And even the *varenyky*[2] she prepared after they drove to grandmother on Sundays and cooked for the whole family. Her *varenyky* were crude, but her mother and her grandmother acted as if they were all right and praised her. Or they let her slice the bacon so as to make the greaves.

Nelja became very upset whenever she thought that she didn't know what Iwasyk usually is doing on weekends when he had no school and no homework. That she didn't know what he was thinking about when he was getting up or was about to fall asleep and what he was dreaming about. What he looked like while asleep or sitting in front of the computer. Whenever they are having Skype, he was always formal and distant, he wanted to look older, to impress her, to show that everything was going well. She would've preferred that he not keep everything to himself, that he would tell her as he used to do when he ran to her previously and buried his head on her breast and complained about someone who had taken away his toys or had been mean to him. And she had stroked his head and kissed his wet eyes, full of tears. But Iwasyk had not been this four-year-old boy anymore. No hard feelings, Nelja thought, for she had also not told him in the end about how out of place she had felt during the first few months in Italy, as she passed every free minute she had on Sundays in the playground nearby like a criminal on the scene of her deed. She sat on a bench, observing the child-

---

2 TN: Ukrainian speciality: Dumplings made with various fillings.

ren, hiding behind a newspaper, and crying softly. Once a little girl came up to her, looked at her curiously and asked in Italian: "What is written in your newspaper: 'Make weepy-weepy?'"

The short phone calls she could afford made matters only worse.

The little son was completely confused at first, and when he got used to it and said, " dear mummy, please come back soon," her money had run out, and the phone was tooting wildly. She hated everything that had left her no choice but to come here and work, she also despised herself for not knowing how to help herself, she despised her illegal existence that didn't allow even a short visit home out of the question. No one would give her back that open, honest boy who so comically shouted "my-my Mom," wrapping his arms around her neck, or looking up at her so pleadingly whenever he wanted to "get up there." He was growing up without her having been a real mother to him. "Meaningless, those memories!," Nelja thought and shooed away her thoughts. What remained to exchange with her son was a few arid messages that looked something like this:

"Call ended. Duration 11:45."

"No answer from Iwan2002."

"Missed call from Iwan2002."

And in between a couple of Iwasyk's smileys. Above all, the one with the little bear, who at the end of the conversation seemed to say "my-my." Iwasyk called him "Embracmi." That was all he showed as emotion, anything more would embarrass him. Otherwise, they talked about the usual, "Do you have enough to eat – what's up in the school – how's Grandma - how's the weather." That was what her father's had taught."Limit yourself to the essentials, don't block the line forever," he had admonished her as a child and had also taught it to his grandson. Her father was now dead for two years already, but that had remained of him: limit yourself to the essential, don't deviate.

Nelja often reflected over what was essential then (whoever works with their hands, has plenty of time to think). How do you know what is really important? Often what was superfluous for one was the most important thing for the other. Previously, before her time in Italy, she had always asked him in the morning what he had been dreaming of, and he readily told her. Now such a question would embarrass him, and he would be put her off, "it's too long to tell, why do you ask so stupid questions." Once, when Nelja was a child, her mother went away for a few days on a business trip. On her return, she found Nelja in tears. She still recalls crying desperately all day long and getting offended with her mum. "I dreamed you were dead, and then you were not there." What worried most Nelja about her son was that he would have no one to talk with, if he dreamed something very bad or someone had angered him, and that this grievance would then always stand between them and intensify with each passing day. And finally become so great that they could no longer get close to one another.

"O paura!" Nelja whispered each night and peered into the most remote and darkest corner of the room. As if *paura* sat there, the giant spider, with whom she wanted to talk. Although there really couldn't be any spiders, for she painstakingly cleaned, and there had never been any complaints. Neither in the last household nor here. Yet, she would never kill a spider, but she would take hold of it with the broom or the cloth and then shake it off in a safe place. That's how her grandmother had always gone about it. At first, Nelja thought her grandmother believed that spiders brought luck or money into the household. "Nonsense," her grandmother explained to her, "whatever is alive, wants to live." "And what if I'm afraid?" Nelja asked. "This fear can be overcome. Just imagine that it's someone you've got to save."

Nelja still winced whenever a spider came right in front of her nose or suddenly dropped onto her hair or on her neck. But as soon as she pulled herself together – Nelja knew that – she could save it, she just pushed it onto something and quickly took it outside. "O paura," Nelja prayed to the giant spider, "I will not kill your children." Grandma Maria had once told her about a spider, which had spun a web in Jesus's burial chamber or that of some other saint, so that no evil people would find him. "O paura," Nelja contemplated, "shield my boy and mother from all evil as long as I'm away and cannot protect them." In that way she imagined her son as a little boy and her mother as a young and pretty woman.

"The people we left behind are no longer the same any more," Wasylyna told her when they met, and told her how it was in reality:

One day comes the point that you abandon everything and head back to your family. You don't let your loved ones know anything about it, it should be a surprise. You inform the family where you're employed, find a replacement, nervously put the last few work days behind you, and every free minute run from one shop to the next to get presents. The whole time you imagine how it will be, how happy they all will be. You give away the few belongings with which you had made to with over the last seven years to your acquaintances. In your thoughts, you take your leave from everything you've had to deal with, from the nice ones and those less so. You're thinking about how much you'll miss everything, but at home you'll be needed more, because your life and your children are there. At the border, the Ukrainian official will wrangle 20 euros out of you, but what can you do, that's how the officials in this country stay afloat, there's nothing to be done about it. Your almost grown-up children will be happy that you've come and above all, that you've brought gifts along. When they hear that you don't want to go back, joy will turn and become pretence. There's no place in the cupboard for your things. All the rooms and closets are already occupied. There's no place for you, the family is used to life without you. For them you're the envelop with money, the umpteen hundred-euro transfers, the voice on the phone that one asks to send this or that, you're the wish fulfilment machine. Your son glares at you whenever you tell him that the new, expensive mobile phone is an unnecessary purchase as long as the old one still works. Your daughter pulls a face and lets you know that she is not going to wear those cheap Chinese and Turkish rags lying around the market stalls. Oh well, it's absolutely your fault, because you, yourself always gave for the kids only the latest, the most shining, the most beautiful, and you've always kept it that way. And you've denied yourself everything. You've treated your toothache with bacon compresses. What the dentist would have cost, 100 euros at least, could be put to better use on the children. That your teeth are in dreadful shape isn't their problem. After a few months you realize that there's no place for you here, that they don't need you here with your problems and notions. They accuse you alone of being responsible for everything they lack; "I'm guilty for them being who they are," you think to yourself. You can't take it anymore and go away, because if you stay, you'll lose you mind. So says Wasylyna. She was lucky. She has a new family here. She has new children here. The other children, as Iwasyk said on the phone, stayed there. Nelja is afraid that Iwasyk will become as bitter as those children are. Nelja is afraid that everything Wasylyna says is true.

In the dark Nelja whispers her "O paura."

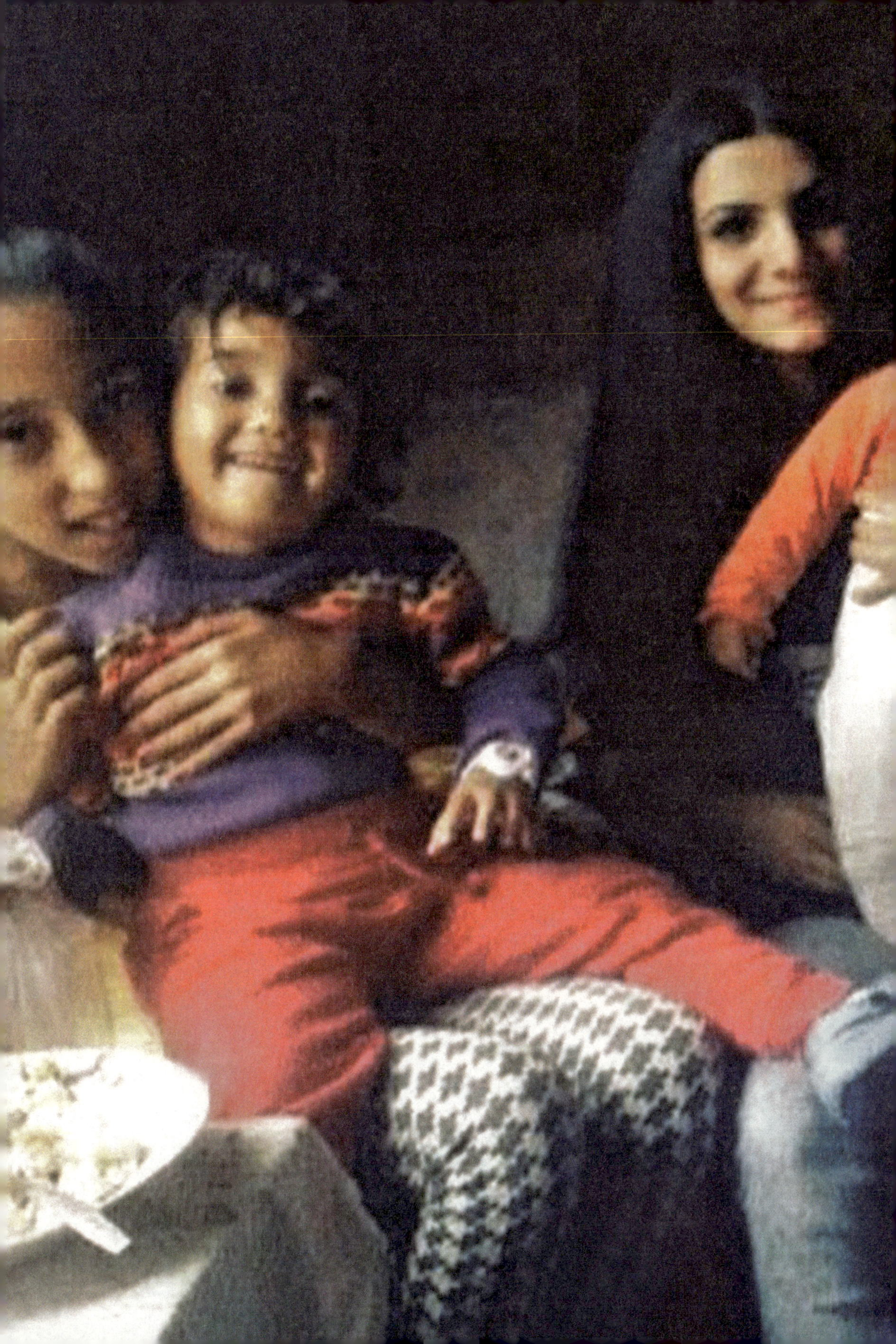

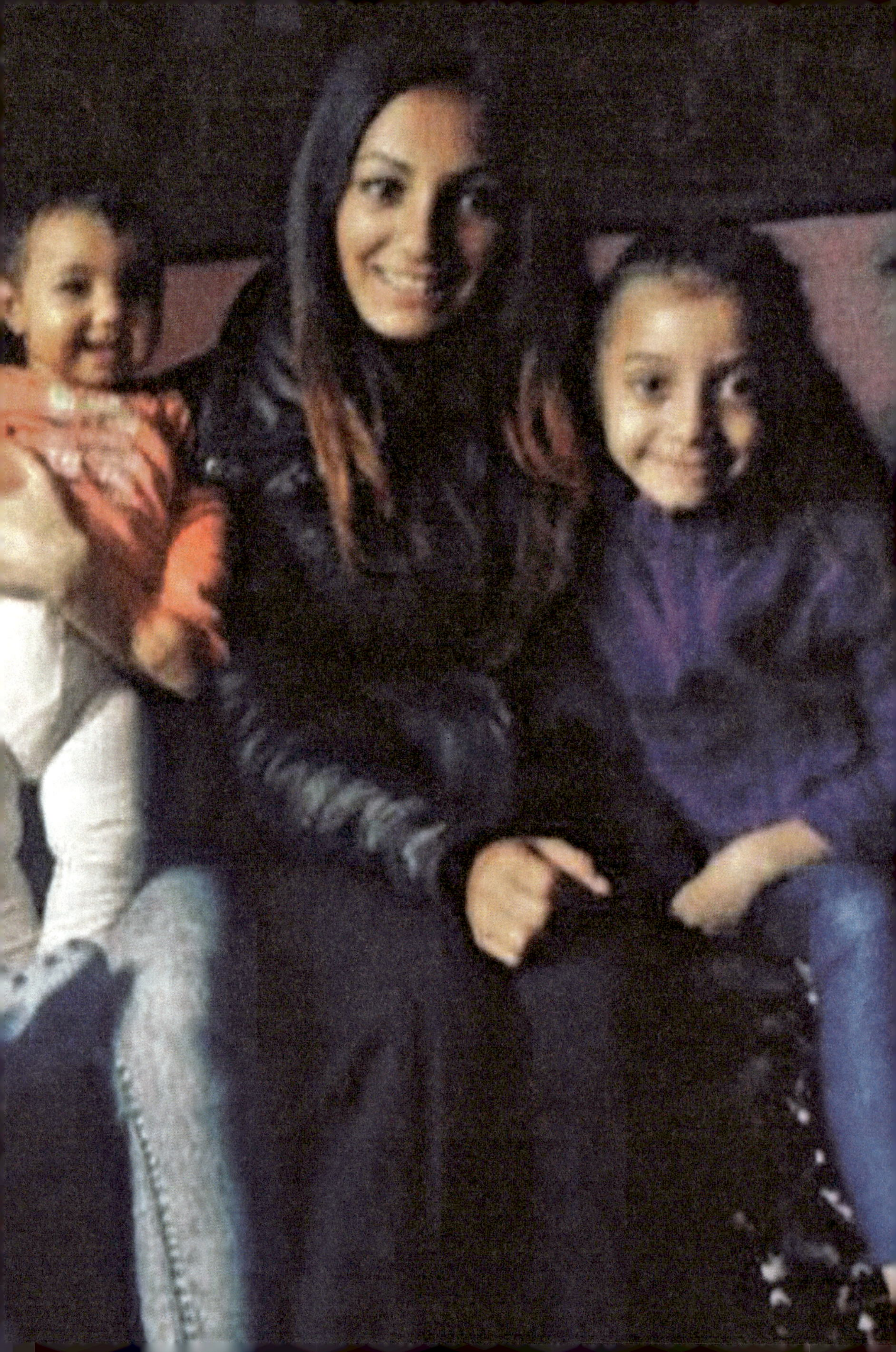

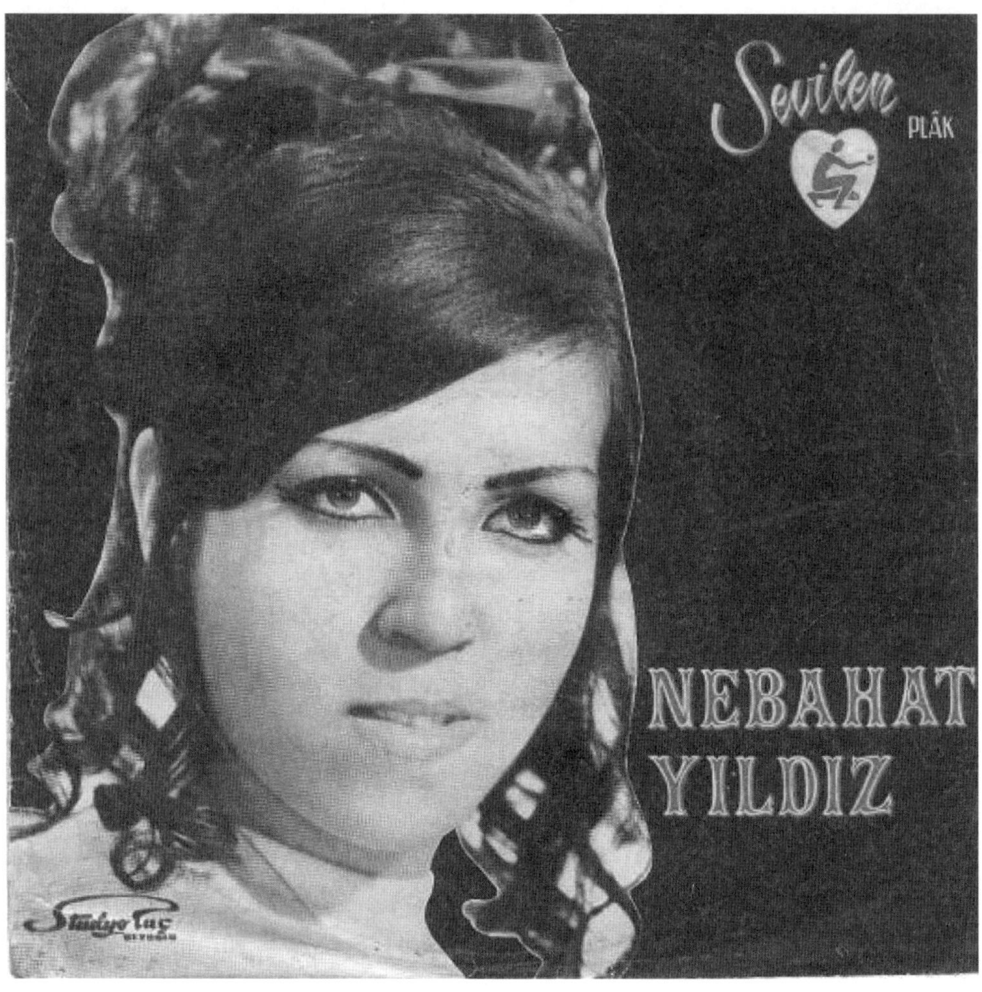

Nebahat Yıldız, a Turkish folk singer, recorded several vinyl records between 1968 and 1974. Later, some of her folk songs (*türkü*) were also released on audio cassettes in Germany. Without knowing whether she had her own migrant experience, we can assume that she used to sing this song following the trend in the 1970s, when many Turkish singers and songwriters began to release songs about the Turkish migration experience.

Germany, Give us our Father Back
Babamızı gönder Almanya

Nebahat Yıldız, 1970's

(Çocuklar ağlıyor)
Anneciğim babamız ne zaman Almanyadan gelecek?
Babanız Almanya'nın yolunu tuttu.
Bizi unuttu
Ağlamayın, günler geçer.
Bir gün babanız döner
Ağlamayın!
Ağlama yettim yavrum ağlama!
(Anne de ağlıyor)

(The children are crying)
Mum, when will our Dad come back from Germany?
Our father has gone to Germany
and forgotten us.
Don't cry, the time will pass.
Your father will come back one day.
Don't cry!
Don't cry, my orphan child, don't cry!
(Mum is crying)

Almanya babamızı sen geri gönder
Üç yavru bir dul ana yolunu gözler
Yalvarıyor öksüzler
Almanya vah Alamanya
Yazıktır üç yetim yavruya
Bağrı yanık garip anaya

Germany, give us our father back
Three kids and one widow are waiting for him
The orphans are begging
Germany, oh Germany!
Have pity on these three kids
And this poor mother whose heart is burning

Yüz mektup oldu yazdım, hiç cevap vermez
Başka sevgili bulmuş dediler gelmez
Gözlerinden yaş dinmez
Almanya vah Alamanya
Yazıktır üç yetim yavruya
Bağrı yanık garip anaya

I wrote a hundred letters, and not one reply
He's found another woman and won't come back, they say.
I'll cry forever
Germany, oh Germany!
Have pity on these three kids
And this poor mother whose heart is burning

Perişan halimizi görenler ağlar
Altı yıldır anamız karalar bağlar
Aramızda dağlar var
Almanya vah Alamanya
Yazıktır üç yetim yavruya
Bağrı yanık garip anaya

Those who see our misery are crying
For six years our mom has been in mourning
There are mountains between us
Germany, oh Germany!
Have pity on these three kids
And this poor mother whose heart is burning

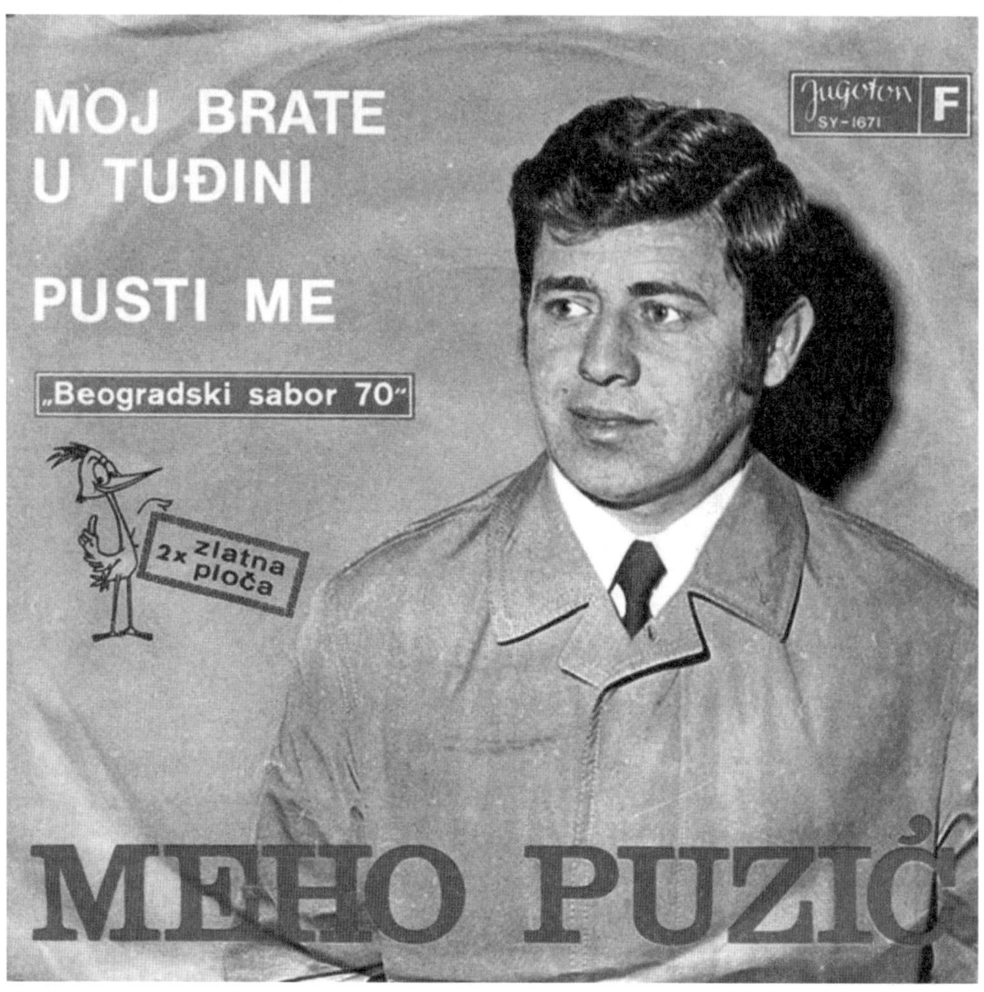

Meho Puzić was a Bosnian folk singer. His song *Moj brate u tuđini* (1970) was one of the first *Gastarbeiter* songs released two years after the bilateral recruitment agreement between West Germany and Yugoslavia.

My Brother
in Foreign Lands
Moj Brate u tuđini

Meho Puzić, 1971

Moj brate u tuđini	**My brother in foreign lands**
piši nam kad ćeš doći	**write us when you will come home**
stara se majka brine	**Our elderly mother worries**
tiho plače svake noći	**and quietly cries at night**
Djeca i draga tvoja	**Your children and your darling**
zovu te, zovu svake noći	**call you, call you every night**
oh brate, dragi brate	**Oh brother, dear brother**
piši nam kad ćeš doći	**write to us when you will come**
Oh tata, dragi tata	**"Oh Dad, dear Dad"**
stalno te zovu tako	**they call you so**
vrati se domu svome	**Return home**
jer djeci nije lako	**because it's not easy for the children**
Oh dođi, dođi brate	**Oh come back, come back, brother**
domu ti, rodnoj grudi	**to your home, to your native land**
srca te naša zovu	**Our hearts call out to you**
sa nama vječno budi	**to be with us forever**

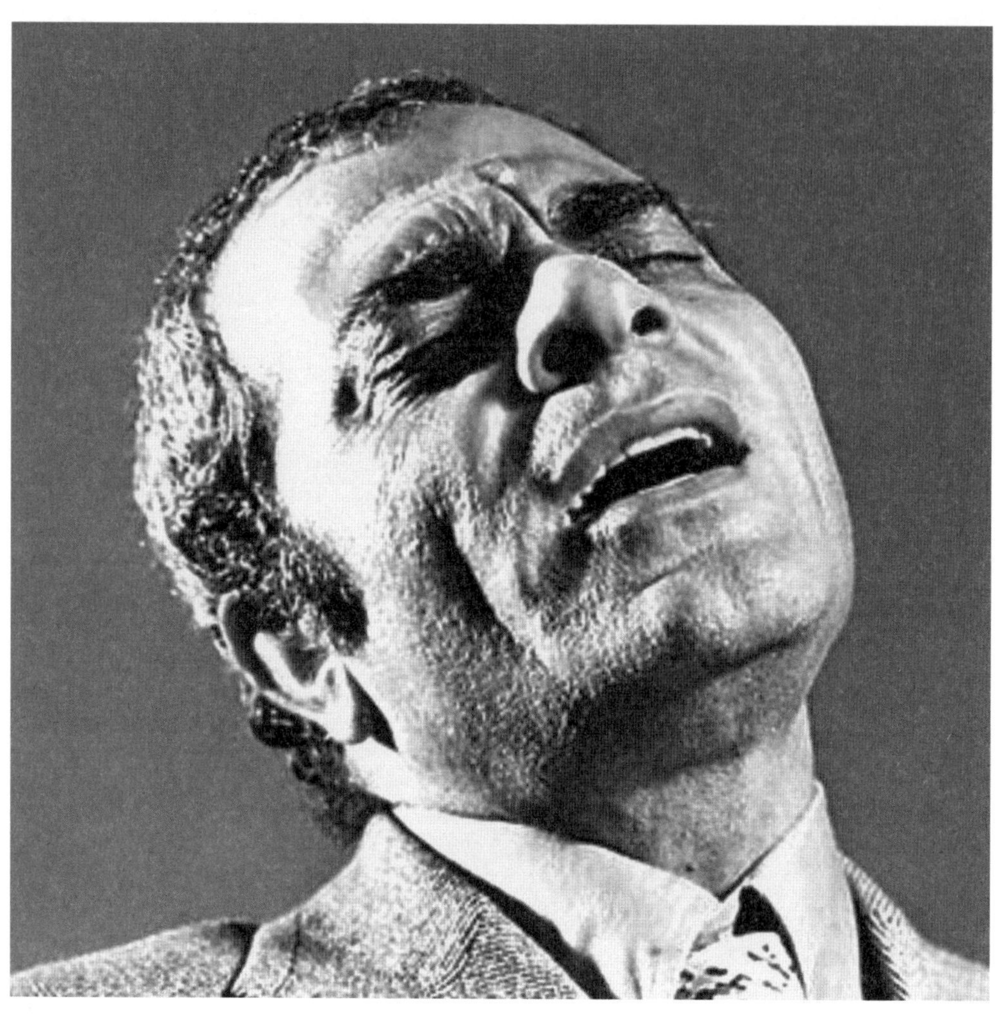

Stelios Kazantzidis (Στέλιος Καζαντζίδης, 1931– 2001) is considered among Greece's most successful singers of the 20th century. In many of his songs he sings of *Xenitiá* – the unknown. With the term *Xenitiá* Kazantzidis links the suffering and longing of those forced to work abroad and those of family members left behind.

The Bread of Foreign Lands
Το ψωμί της ξενιτιάς

Stelios Kazantzidis, 1975

Το ψωμί της ξενιτιάς είναι πικρό
το νερό της θολό και το στρώμα σκληρό
τα λεφτά που αποκτάς τα βλαστημάς
υποφέρεις πονάς την πατρίδα ζητάς

Κλέφτρα ξενιτιά τα παλικάρια κλέβεις
μάγισσα κακιά με τα λεφτά μαγεύεις
πάντα μ' απονιά χωρίζεις μάνες και παιδιά

Κάνε Παναγιά η ξενιτιά να πάψει
κι άλλη μάνα πια για χωρισμό μην κλάψει
κι όλα τα παιδιά στο σπίτι τους να 'ρθουν
ξανά

Το ψωμί της ξενιτιάς είναι ξερό
και με δάκρυ πικρό το 'χω βρέξει κι εγώ
πιο καλά στο φτωχικό ψωμί κι ελιά
παρά χίλια καλά στην πικρή ξενιτιά

Κλέφτρα ξενιτιά τα παλικάρια κλέβεις
μάγισσα κακιά με τα λεφτά μαγεύεις
πάντα μ' απονιά χωρίζεις μάνες και παιδιά

Κάνε Παναγιά η ξενιτιά να πάψει
κι άλλη μάνα πια για χωρισμό μην κλάψει
κι όλα τα παιδιά στο σπίτι τους να 'ρθουν
ξανά

The bread of foreign lands is bitter
its water muddy, its bed hard
you curse the money you earn / you suffer,
you ache, you ask for your homeland

Furtive foreign lands you steal our young
men / bad magic! you bewitch us with money
you always part mothers and children so
heartlessly

Let the Virgin Mary abandon foreign lands
and no mother cry because of separation
and all the children return to their homes

The bread of foreign lands is dry
bitter tears I have shed upon it
fresh bread and olives in the humble home
than thousands of goods in those bitter
foreign lands

Furtive foreign lands you steal our young men
bad magic! you bewitch us with money
you always part mothers and children so
heartlessly

Let the Virgin Mary abandon those foreign
lands / and no mother cry because of
separation / and all the children return to
their homes

Mickey Bustos (born 1981) is a Filipino-Canadian singer and comedian
who became famous through the TV show *Canadian Idol*. His song
Balikbayan Box – a parody on Miley Cyrus' song and video *Wrecking Ball*
– refers to the so called "homecoming boxes" or "repatriate boxes" which
Filipino workers abroad can send their families home duty- and tax-free,
due to a law passed in 1987. The boxes are filled with goods, which are
not necessarily difficult to find in the Philippines, such as non-perishable
food, toiletries, household items, electronics, toys, designer clothing.

**"Whether it be coming from Canada, USA, Dubai, Europe, Australia, other
Asian countries, or elsewhere, we Filipinos love to receive a *Balikbayan
Box* from our loved ones abroad! This song is based on a true story!"**

Mickey Bustos Canada/ Philippines

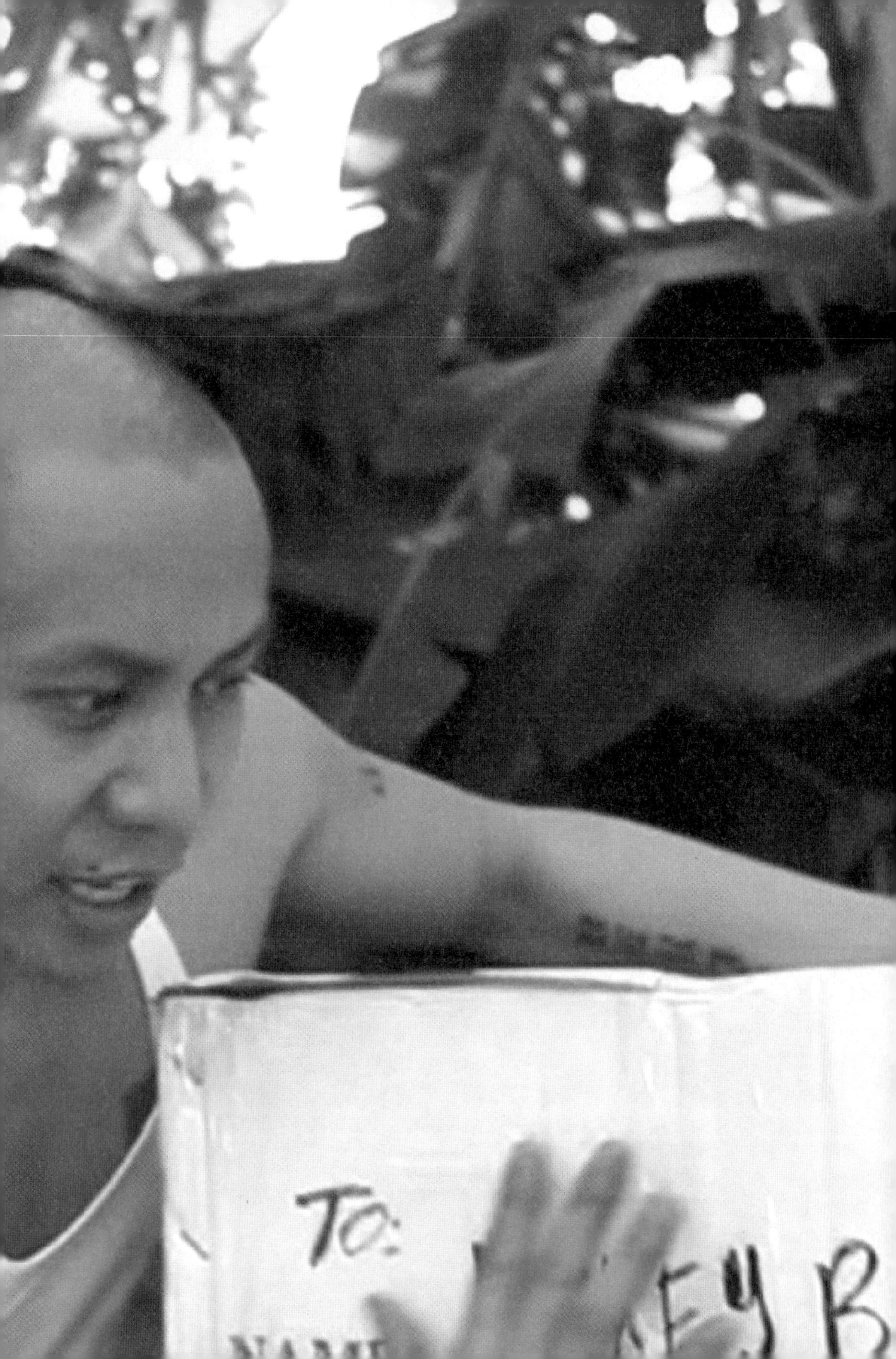
TO:
NAM
EY B

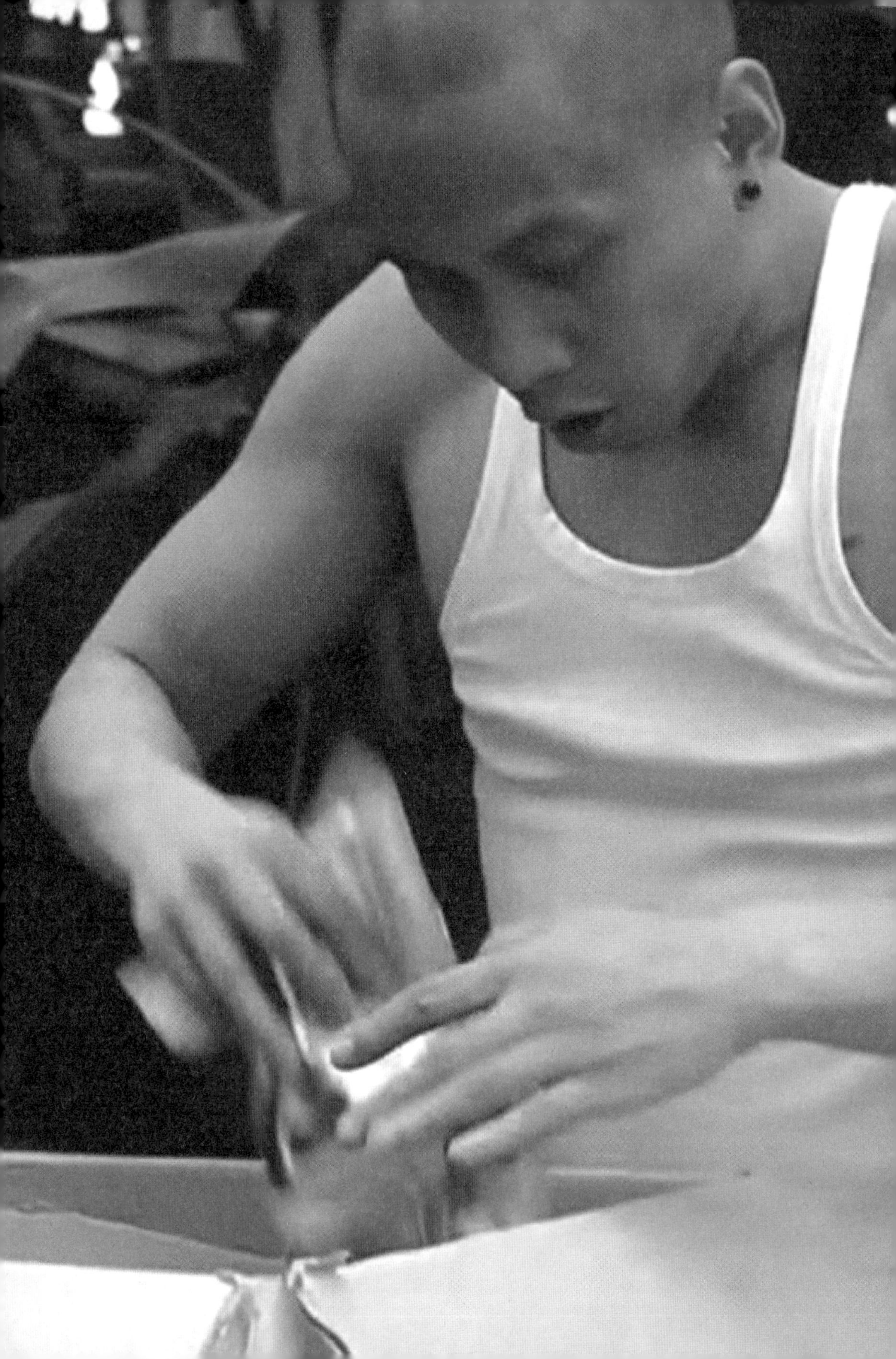

Balikbayan Box

Mickey Bustos, 2013

Hello? Mummy? Ohh, you sending what?

You called and told me *"Anak ko*[1] we
sent you *balikbayan box."* I jumped and
screamed imagining having all those
foreign products!

I'll have Coffeemate, lotion, chocolates,
shampoo even if I'm kalbo, second hand
dammit, I don't care I still want it, as long
as there's brand name to show!

I'm getting a balikbayan box, sent to me
from my Mom abroad.
I will wait for whole 2 months, all those
pasalubong[2] coming to me,
and I am hoping for Canadian money.

I waited for your door to door, it came, I
handled it with care.
"It's heavy" Frank said so excited to smell
that North American air.
But there was so much tape, I could not
open it, and a rope tied around the whole
box. The address is written everywhere
as if we're blind over here and OA naman
yung padlocks.

I got my balikbayan box, I waited for it for
2 months. I bet it's full of awesome stuff.
Some Colgate and new briefs, imported
corn beef, I got my balikbayan box,
so full of imported products,
I know I will feel so *sosyal*[3] *parang*
foreigner lang, thanks to my Mommy.
I'll have Nikes on my feet!
After using lots of force, I finally managed
to get it in.
There's so much newspaper, good
Lord, about Toronto Mayor Robert Ford.

Excited for the gifts within, I started to dig
deep inside,
and when I finally got in, I just could not
believe my eyes.

I just want to say, to my dear Mommy, I
will always love you.

But I got my balikbayan box and
everything inside sucks,
some medicine for chicken pox, holy
water in case of what? Conjuring?!
You sent oil of oregano (*ano 'to?*)[4] a winter
coat in case it snows (it's so hot),
a pair of sexy panty hose, *ay naku*[5] what
is this? Melted ice cream! And this?
Always with wings! *Ay naku Medyas*[6] that
stinks!

Buhuhuhu…

---

1 Tagalog: My Child

2 Tagalog: [something] for when you welcome
me. In the Philippines it is common to bring
presents from a journey for friends and family
staying back home, especially for children.

3 Tagalog: Slang term for 'upper class'

4 Tagalog: What's this?

5 Tagalog: Slang for 'Oh my God'

6 Tagalog: Socks

Antonia Stoian from Targu Jiu in Romania started her career as a twelve year-old on the "Next Star" show. There she performed her song *Ai plecat mama departe*. Her mother was especially invited as a surprise guest by the Next Star team to assist in the competition. In front of the audience, the moderator and the jury, Antonia hugged her mother, whom she had not seen for two years, for she had been forced to go to Spain to work.

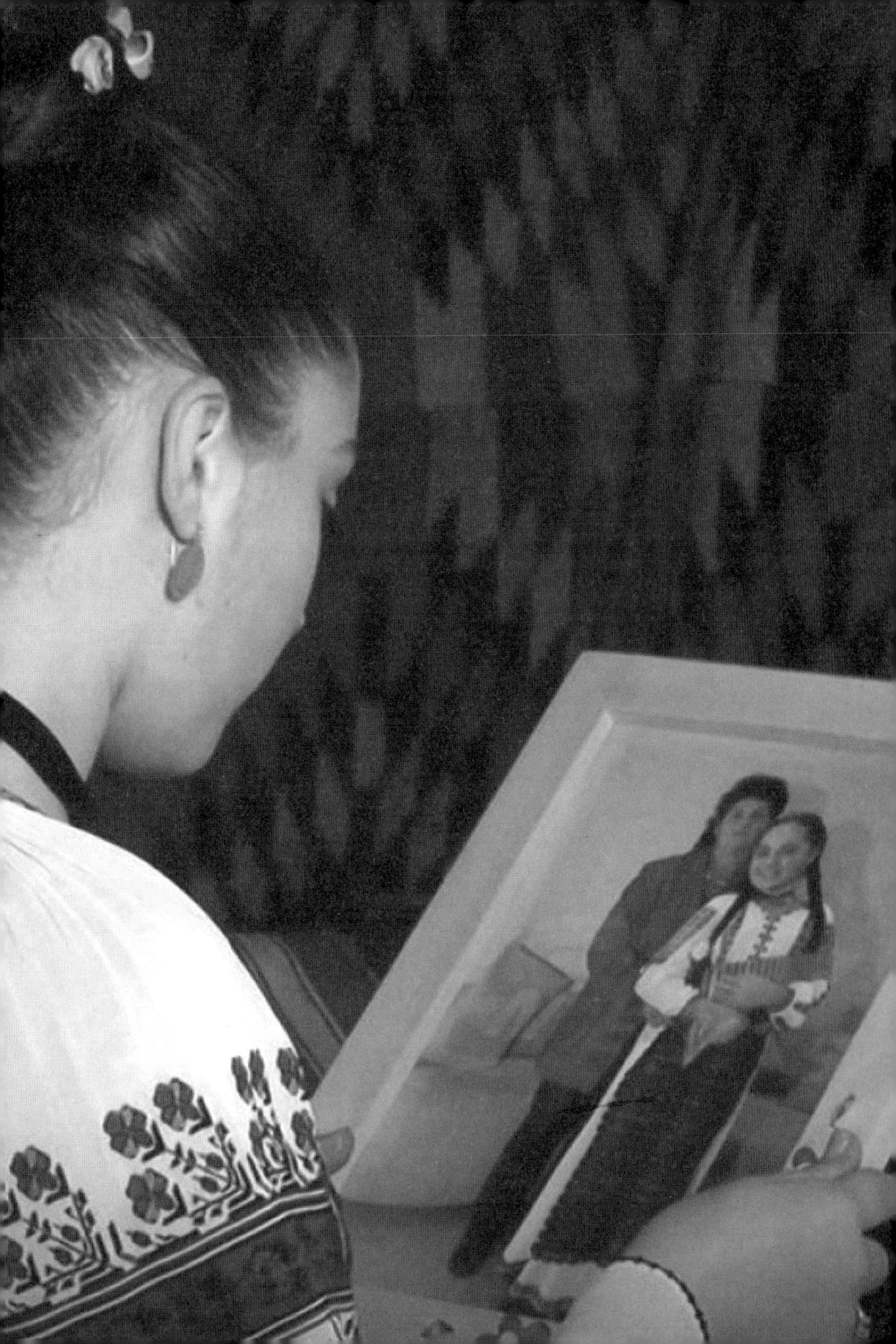

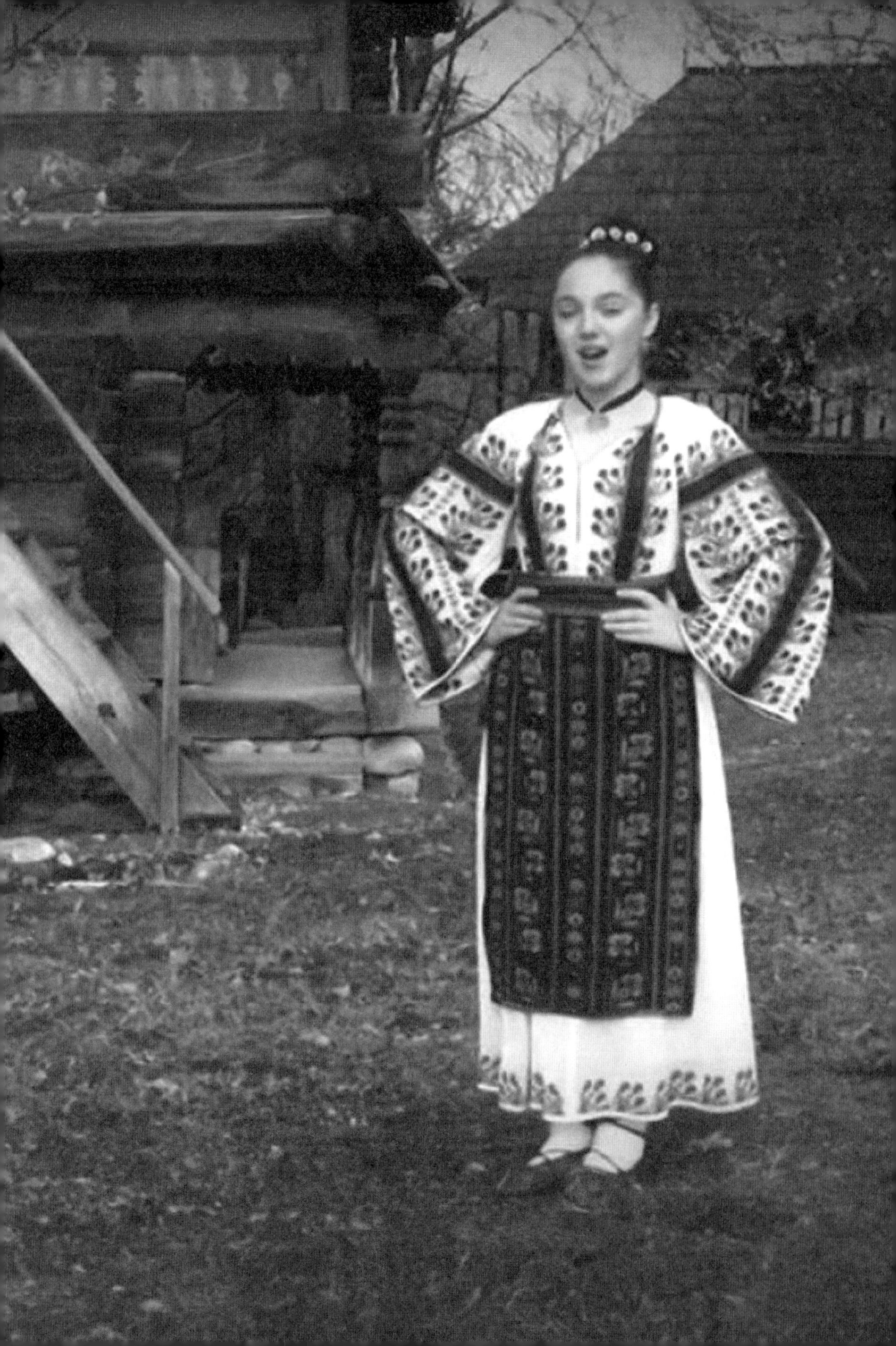

Mother, You've Gone Away
Ai plecat mamă departe

Antonia Stoian, 2011

Ai plecat mamă departe Tea-i dus in străinătate Iar ție nu-ți pasă Tată, Că-i pe lume-o fată.	Mother, you've gone away, far away to that foreign land And you father, you're not interested that You have a girl in this world, waiting for you.
Voi părinții, orice ar fii, Rămâneți lângă copii! Banii nu țin niciodată, Locul de mamă și tată.	You parents, no matter what happens, Stay with your children Money can never replace Mummy and Daddy.
Ce m-aș face, că-s prea mică, Dacă n-aș avea bunică! Ea mereu grija mea poartă, Si plânge de a mea soartă!	What would I do, for I'm still small, Without my Granny! She always looks after me She cries because of my fate
Voi părinții, orice ar fii, Rămâneți lângă copii Banii nu țin niciodată, Locul de mamă și tată	You parents, no matter what happens, Stay with your children! Money can never replace Mummy and Daddy.
Nu vreau bani, să-mi fie bine, Vreau pe mama lângâ mine Poate orice să-mi lipsească, Nu dragostea părintească!	I don't want money for my well-being I want my mother next to me I can do without everything But not without my parents' love!
Voi părinții, orice ar fii, Rămâneți lânga copii, Banii nu țin niciodată, Locul de mamă și tată!	You parents, no matter what happens Stay with your children Money can never replace Mummy and Daddy.

In a private video on YouTube a teenager dedicates a
song to "all those children whose parents work abroad."

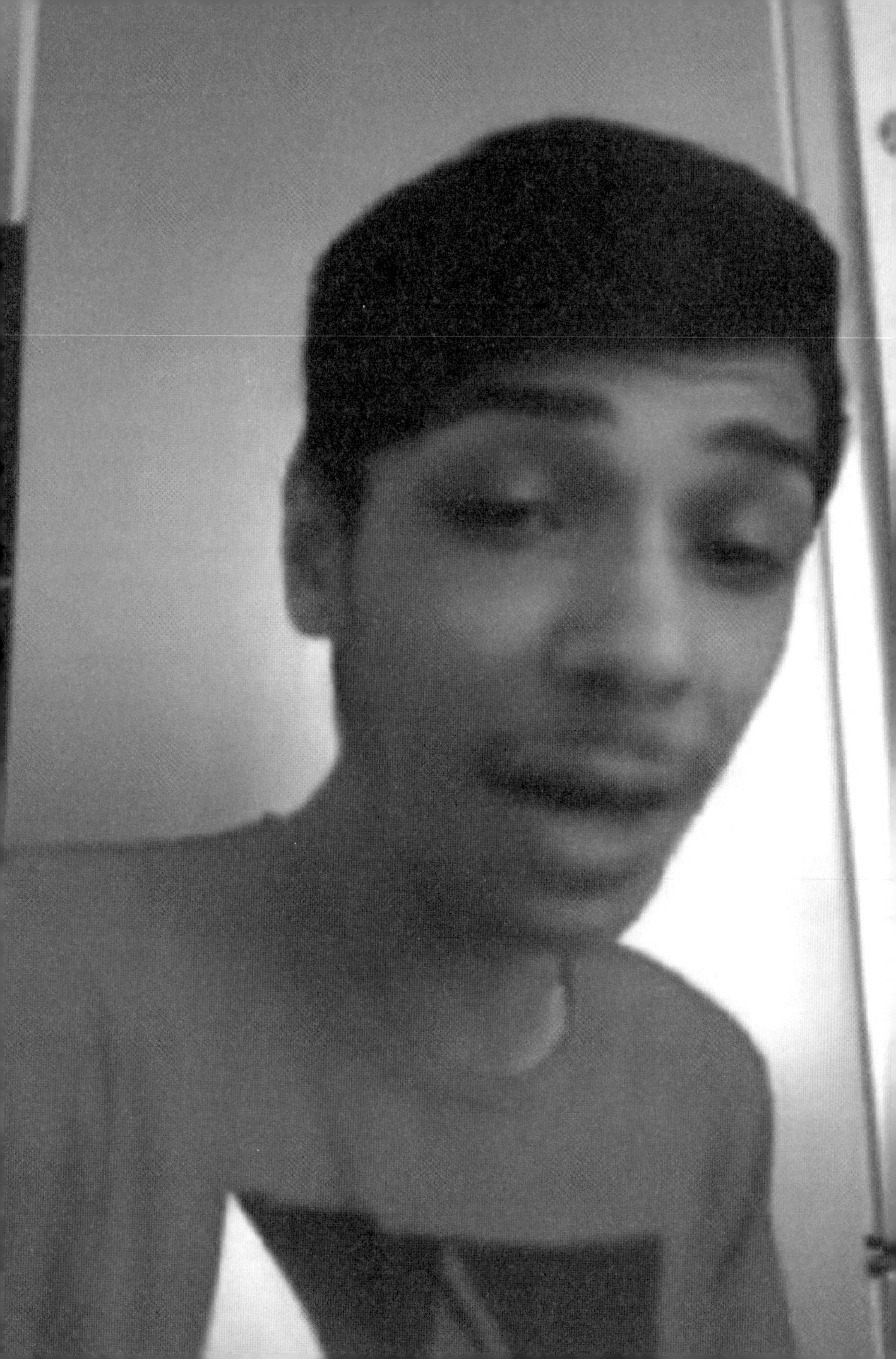

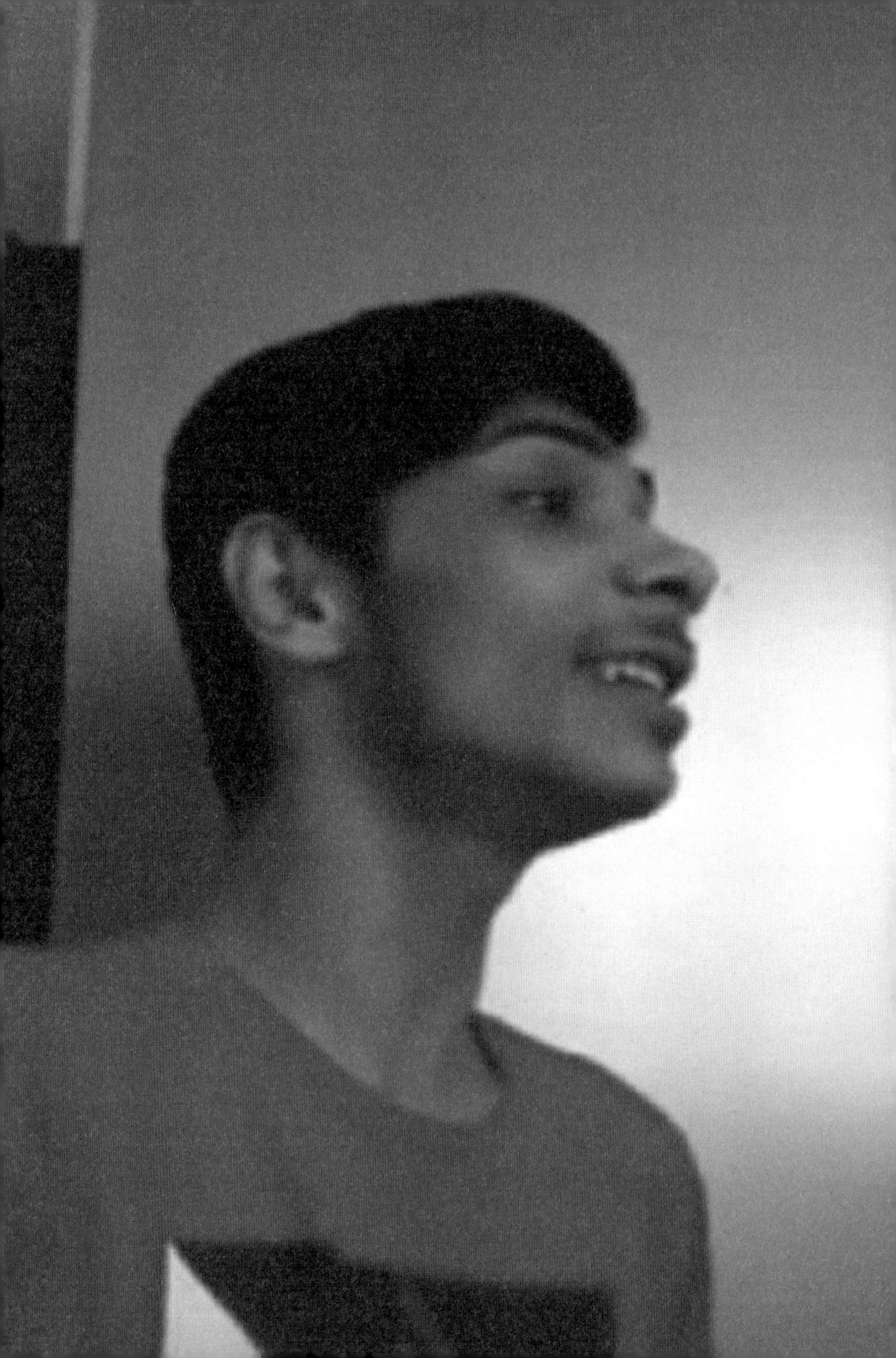

A verse for all those children whose parents work abroad

O strofă pentru copii care au părinții la muncă în străinătate

Unknown, 2016

Seara când mă pun la cină,
Îmi fac cruce cu a mami mână,
Şi mănânc tot singurea,
Cu gândul la mama mea.

Cine face legile,
Ca şi supărările,
La copii nu se gândesc,
Că fără mama lor cresc.

**When I sit down for supper at night,
I make the sign of the cross with my
mother's hand,
And I eat all alone, thinking of my mother.**

**Those making the laws,
and those creating all the troubles,
Don't think of those children,
who have to grow up without their mothers.**

Denisa Manelista (1989 - 2017), whose real name was Denisa Emilia Răducu, was already singing at the age of twelve on various TV shows and conquered Romanian audiences with her traditional Manele songs. Emigration and the suffering of transnational families are such a part of daily life in Romania that the subject also made its way into Manele songs and into pop music.

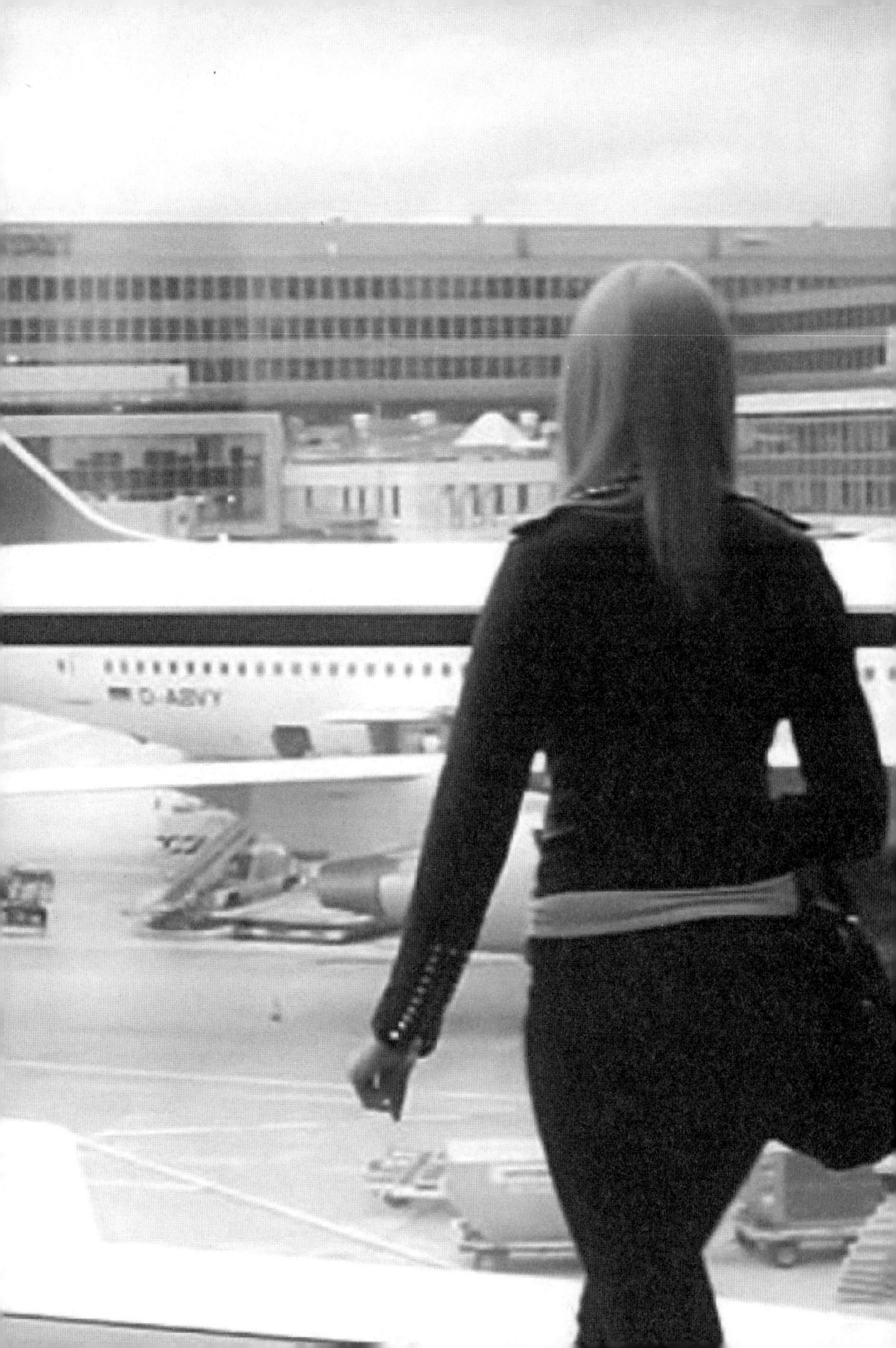

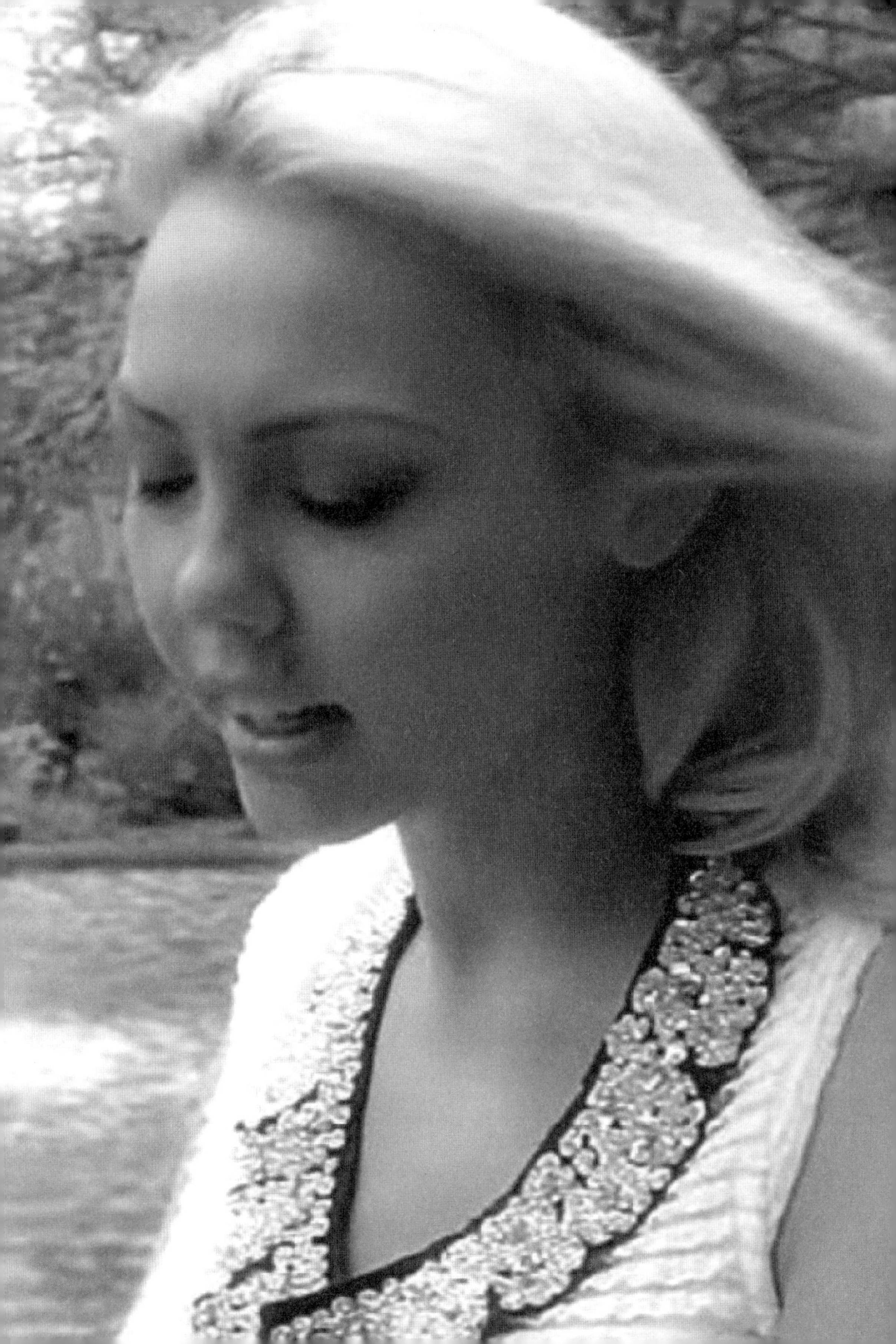

Mother, Wipe My Tears Away
Șterge, mamă, lacrima

Denisa, 2011

Șterge mamă lacrima	Mother, wipe my tears away
Cu colțul de la bazma.	With the corner of your headscarf.
De cinci ani si până acuma	Five years already and still now
Plânge săraca întruna,	She cries endlessly and poor,
De fetița ei ce-o are	Her little girl
Singura prin lumea mare.	Is alone in this big world.
Fir-ai tu, străinătate	Damn you, foreign lands
Ma ți de mama departe	You keep my mother
Și de Crăciun și de Paște	Whether at Christmas or Easter
Mă-ntreb de mă mai cunoaște.	I ask myself whether you still know me.
Săraca măicuță mea	My poor little mother
Cum o fi inima-n ea?	How is it in the depths of her heart?
Alții vin cu toți acasă,	Others come home with everything,
Ea stă singură la masă	While she sits alone at the table
Și multe lacrimi mai varsă.	And sheds so many tears.

Since its independence, Ukraine has increasingly become a supply source for migrant workers. They are heading to Germany, to the new Eastern European EU member states and to southern Europe in search of work. The songs of **Vasyl Danyliuk** and Iryna Lonchyna, as sung by **Violetta Timofieva**, particularly highlight female emigration: many women work in the care sector in the host countries and are forced by circumstances to leave their children behind in Ukraine.

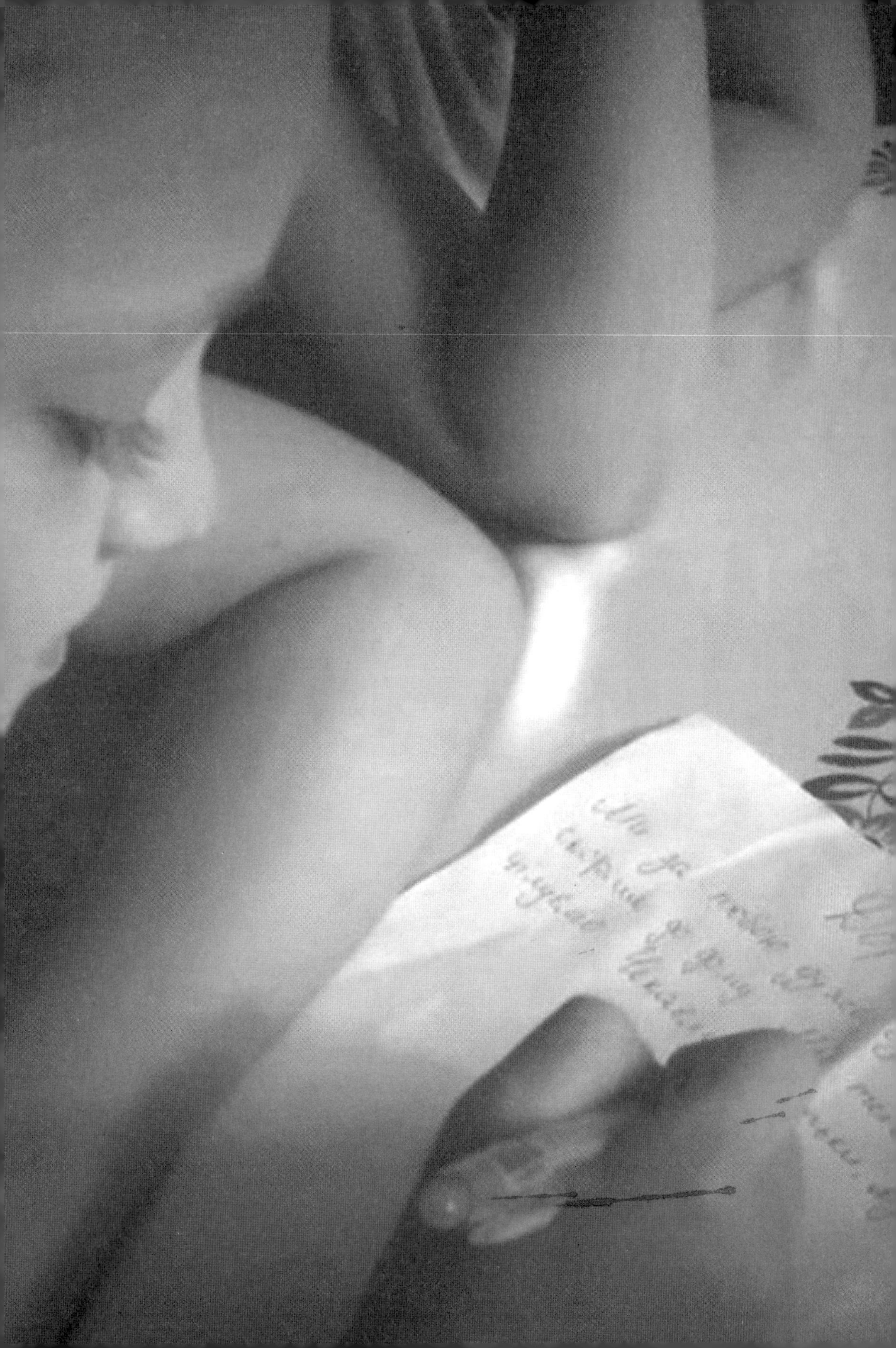

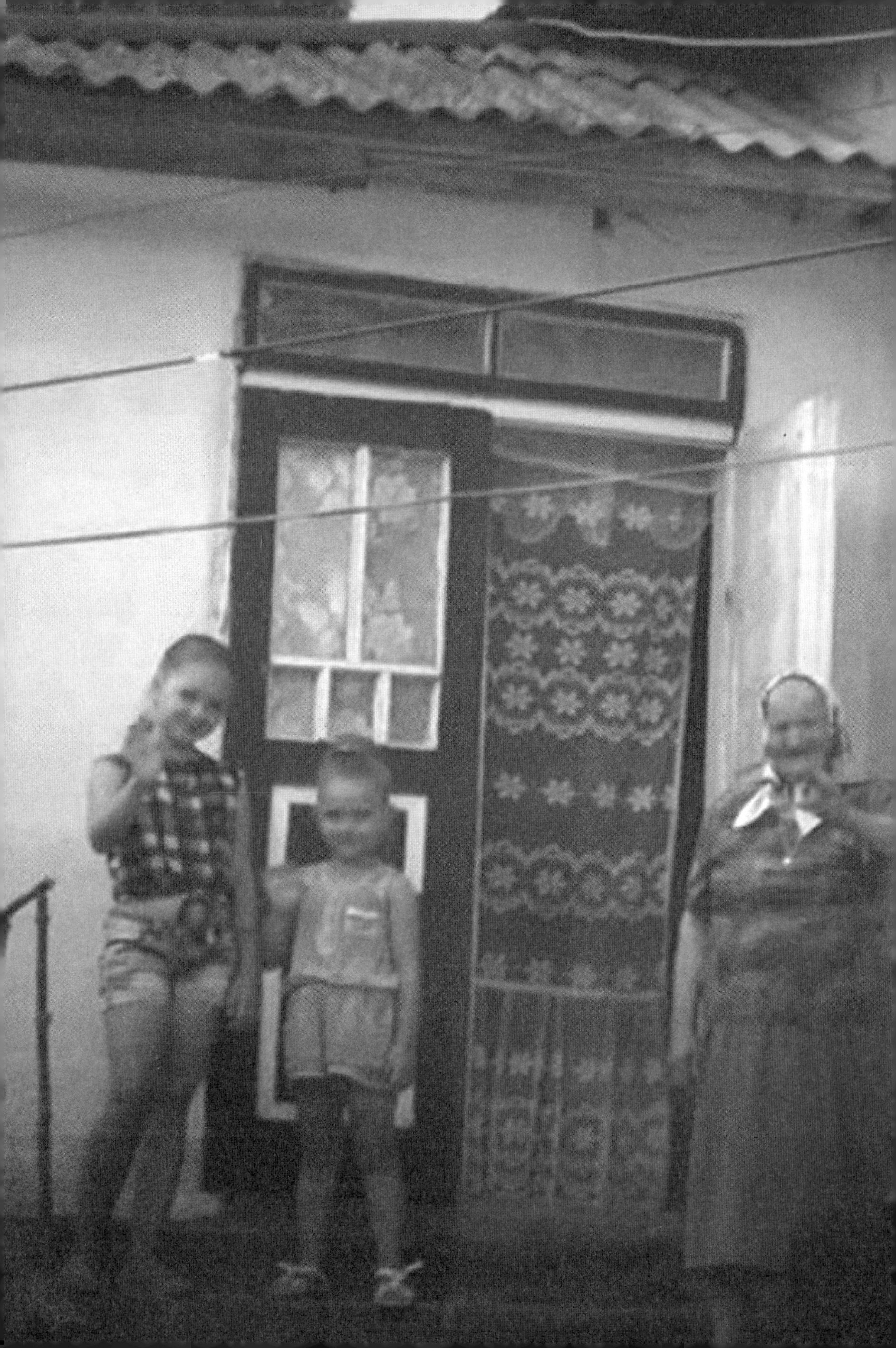

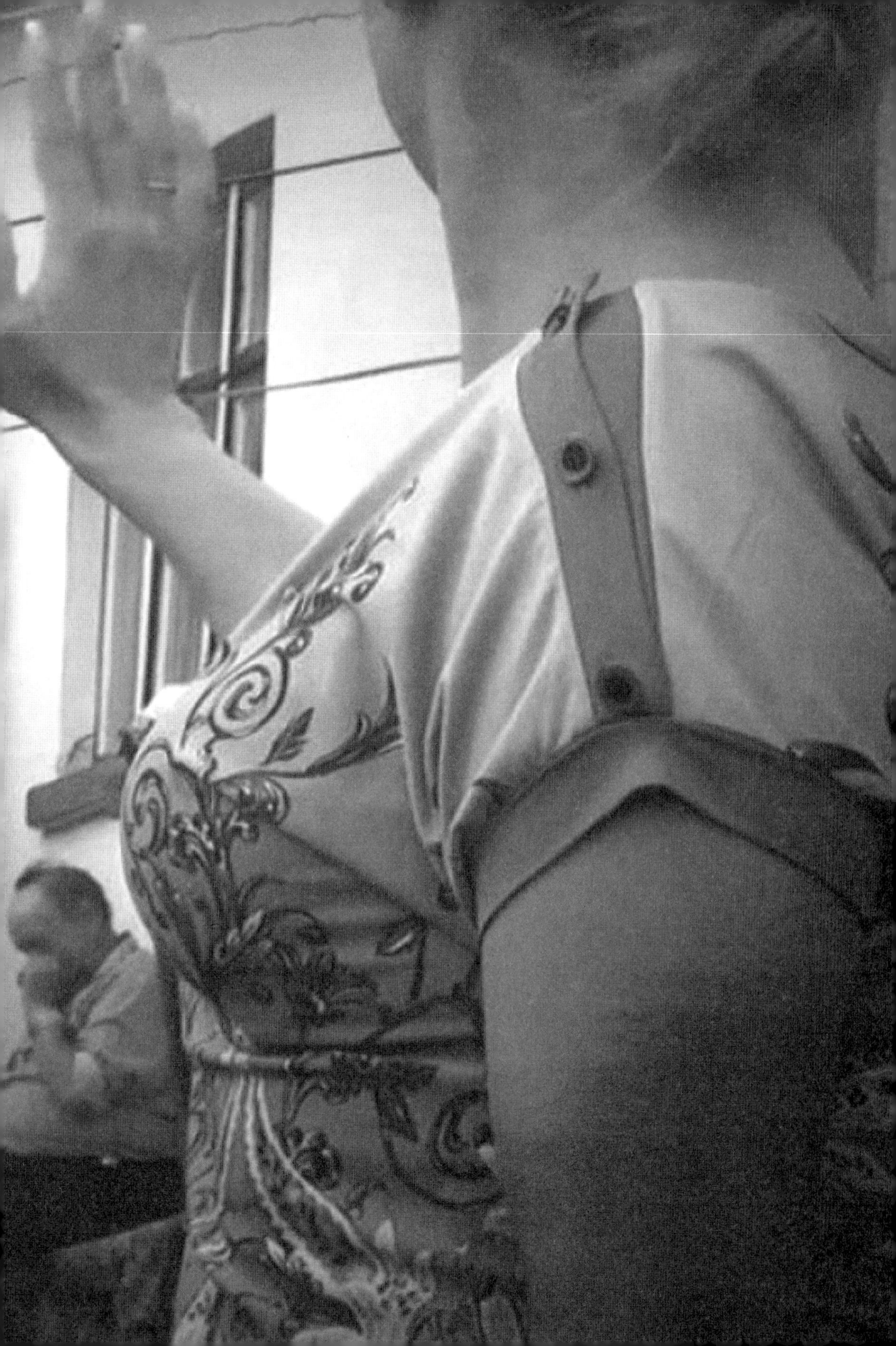

Іронія долі... Історія матері-жінки:
Зібрала валізу і їде в незвіданий край.
Її проводжає родина, неначе навіки...
Куди вона їде? Навіщо? Чому? - Не питай...
Хіба не знайдеться їй місця у рідному домі?
Чому вона тяжко працює на іншій землі?
Поїхала мати у пошуках кращої долі,
Щоб в скруті не жили, не ниділи діти її.

Берегиня роду, мати-українка,
Втратила свободу... За кордоном гірко...
Коротає вік свій на чужій землі,
Ждуть від неї вістку діточки малі...

А діти сумують: їм мамина ласка потрібна,
З вікна виглядають в зажурі старенькі батьки.
Скоріш повертайся додому, матусенько рідна, -
Читає в листах вже до болю знайомі рядки...
Так часто в тривожні хвилини втрачали ми віру,
Губили надію, та не забуваймо одне:
Без матері-жінки ми втратимо і Україну.
Не нація та, що так легко втрачає святе!

Берегиня роду, мати-українка,
Втратила свободу... За кордоном гірко...
Коротає вік свій на чужій землі,
Ждуть від неї вістку діточки малі...

Faraway Mother
Мати-емігрантка

Violetta Timofieva, 2014

Irony of fate ... The story of a mother and of a woman:
She has packed her suitcase and is going to unknown lands.
Where is she going? For what? Why? – Don't ask me ...
Is there no place for her at home?
Why does she work so hard in that faraway land?
Mother went to look for a better future,
For a better life for her children

Family-keeper, faraway mother,
Lost her freedom ... bitter is that faraway land ...
She ages in a foreign land,
Her little children still waiting for some news from her ...

And the children miss her: they need a mother's love.
Her old sad parents are staring out the window,
Please come back home soon, beloved mother, –
With a pain in heart she reads similar lines in their letters ...
So often in the alarming moments we lost our faith,
Lost hope, but we didn't forget one thing:
Without a mother and women, we will lose Ukraine.
A nation that so easily loses holy things can't be a nation!

Family-keeper, faraway mother,
Lost her freedom ... bitter is that faraway land ...
She ages in a foreign land,
Her little children still waiting for some news from her ...
Her little children still wait for a letter from her ...

The name of the song *Заробітчанки* (zarobitchanka) is the Ukrainian
term for "wage-earner" and denotes a female labour migrant who
has to go abroad in search of work, leaving her family and children
behind, in order to earn money for the family upkeep.

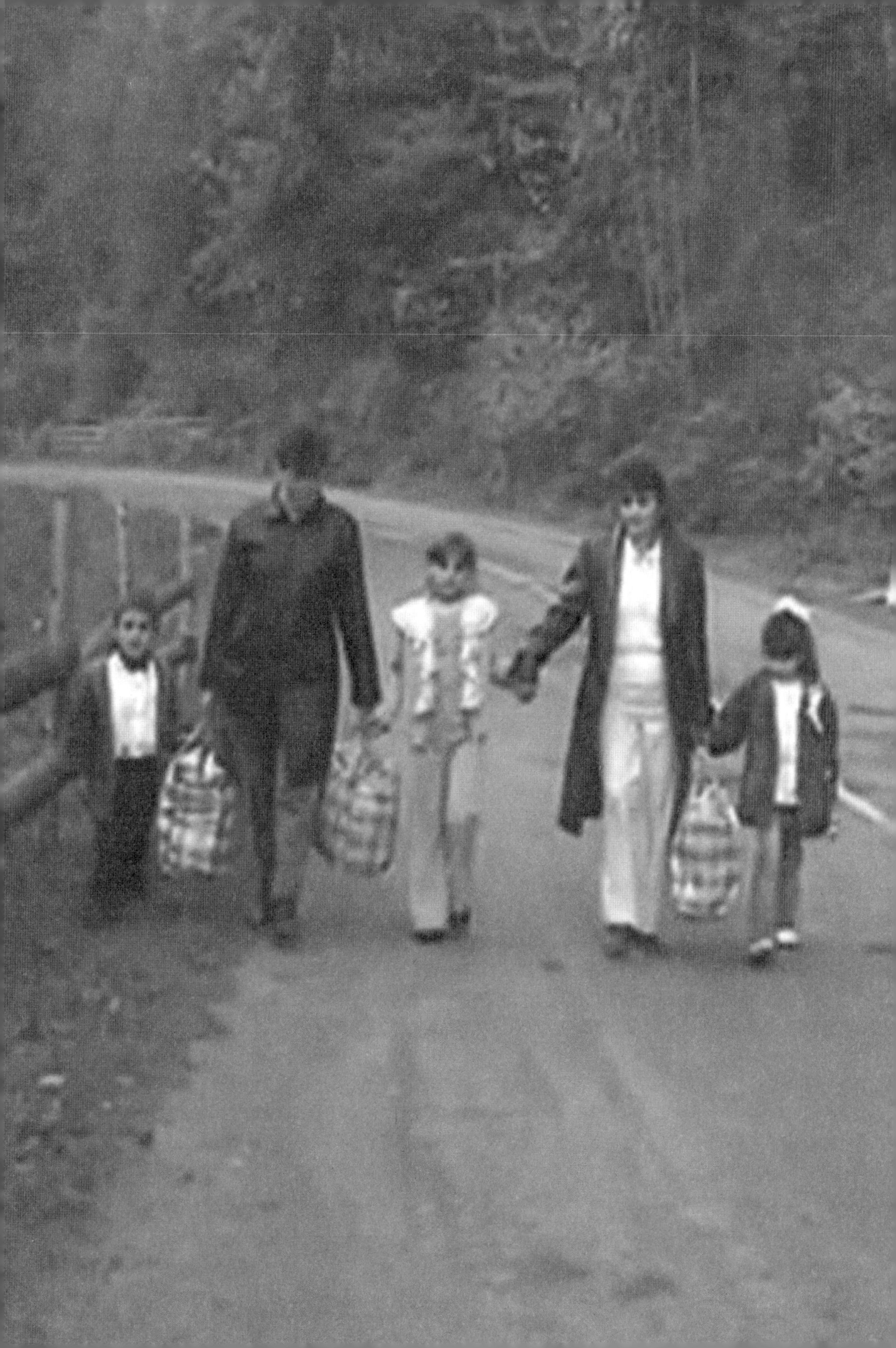

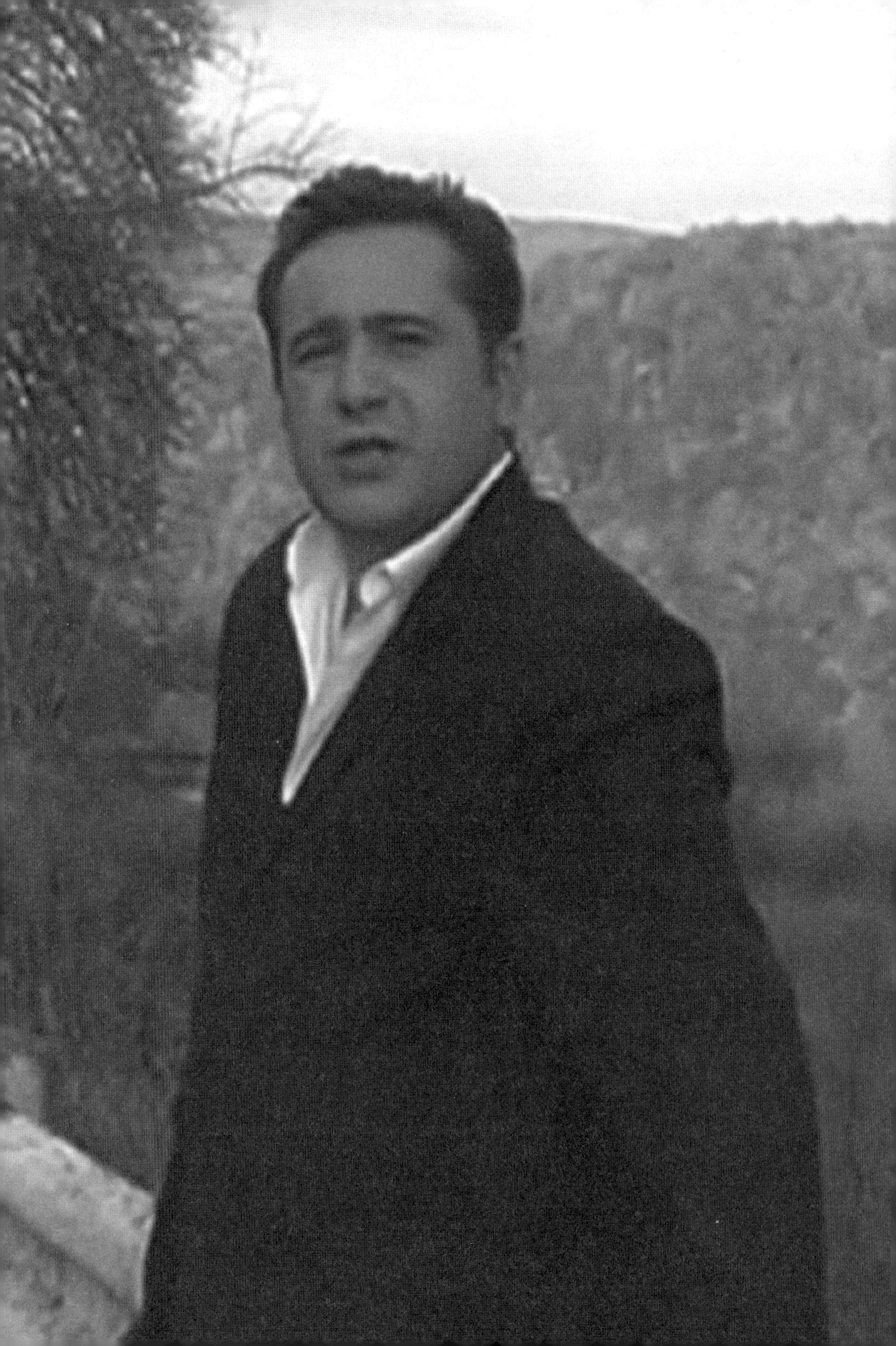

Wage Earner
Заробітчанка

Vasyl Danyliuk, 2007

В жіночій долі смак гіркий,
Хоч залишилися вдома дітки.
Вкраїнські молоді жінки
Із дому йдуть на заробітки.
Далекий і нелегкий шлях,
Десь до Італії і далі
І в заклопотаних очах
Утіхи менше ніж печалі.

Як щастя мало, як щастя мало.
Згадаймо істину стару.
А під вікном чекають маму,
Чекають доню і сестру.
Як сліз багато, як сліз багато.
Чому це сталось — не збагнеш.
А без жінок пустіє хата, а без жінок
пустіє хата.
І рідний край пустіє теж.

Нащо ті гроші — ви скажіть,
Коли розтоптуються душі,
Але людині треба жить
І каже жінка: "Їхать мушу",
І правда ця неначе ніж,
Який виблискує криваво -
Чого ж ти бачиш і мовчиш
Моя розгублена державо?

Female destiny has a bitter taste,
Despite the children staying at home.
Ukrainian young women
Go abroad to earn money.
It's far away and not at all easy,
To Italy and beyond
And in their worried eyes
Little joy and much sorrow.

Such a lack of happiness, such a lack of happiness. / Let's remind ourselves of the old truth.
That under the window someone is waiting for
mom, / Waiting for our daughters and sisters.
How many tears, how many tears.
Why has this all happened – you will never
understand. / And the home is empty without
women, / And the home is empty without
women, / And our Motherland is empty, too.

Why do you need this money – you will ask
When souls are torn asunder,
But humans must survive
And the woman says: "I must go,"
This truth is like a knife
That glistens with blood –
Why do you just look on and remain silent
My confused country?

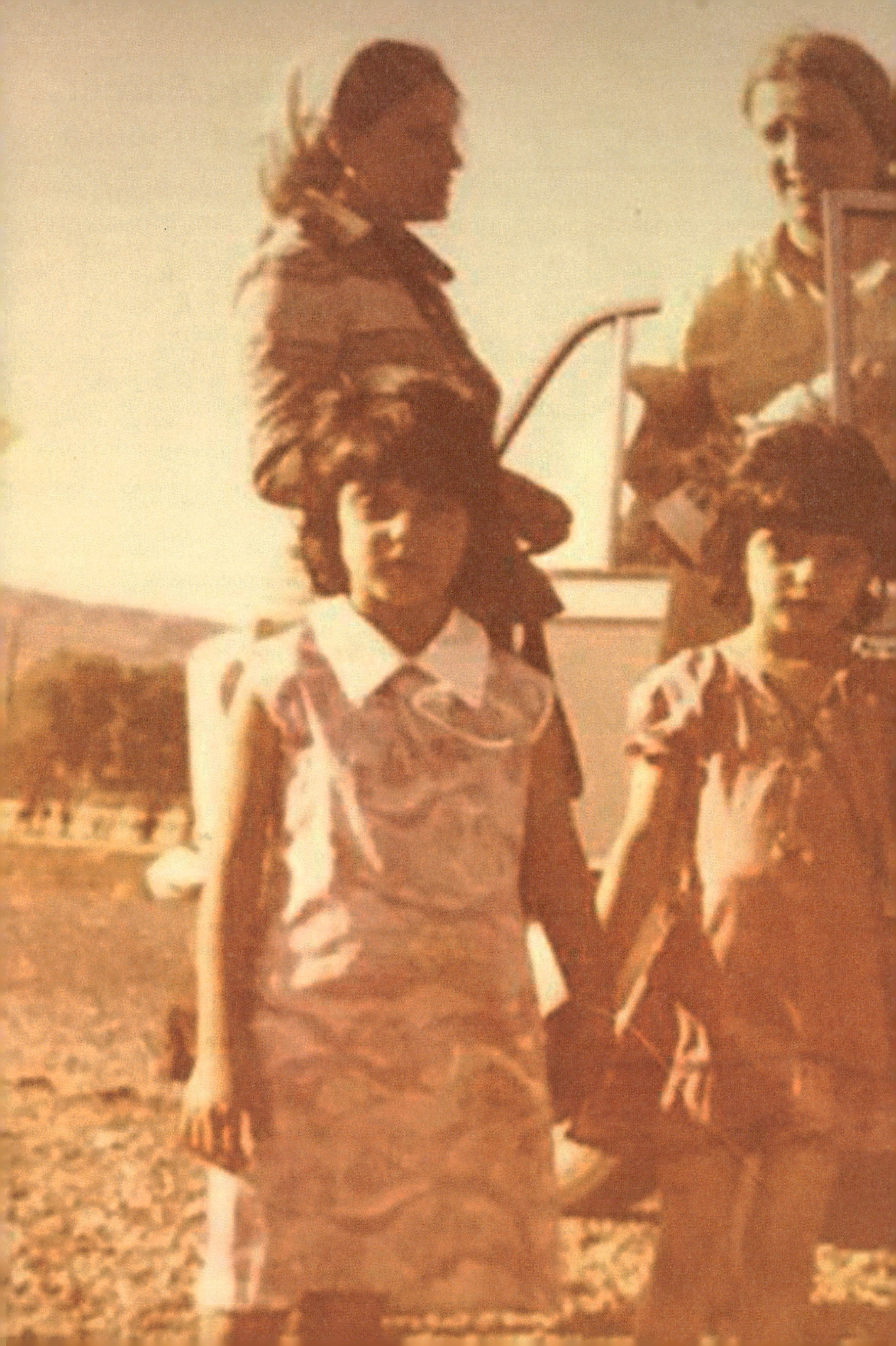

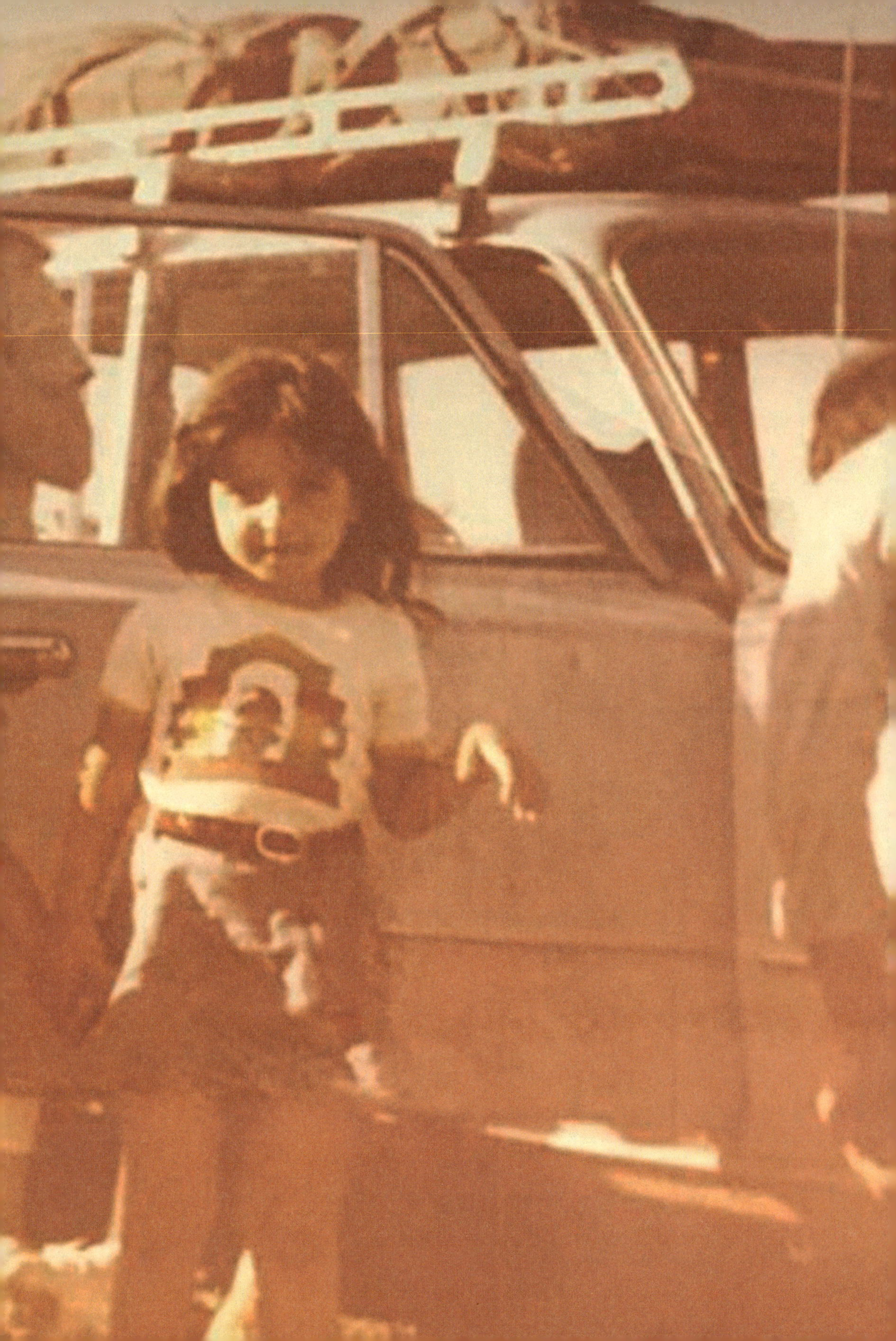

The following interviews were conducted by Malve Lippmann and
Can Sungu in various cities in Germany, Turkey, Romania and Greece.
They are testimonials from children and parents who were or are still
affected by work-related family separation today or at the time of
recruitment. Their memories and stories show the individual motivations
and social conditions that led to the interviewees being separated from
their family. Moreover, the personal feelings and conflicts between
parents and children, as well as the aspect of gifts in the field of tension
of material supply and physical absence become clear.

"Probably the only thing that I haven't yet sent is a real house. I've sent everything else"

Gülnar Istanbul, Turkey

I'm in Turkey already eleven years. I have a twelve-year-old son. I cared for him until he was one year old. Then I left him with my parents. No job. No money. Nothing. No factory. No *zavods*[1] like in the past. There were a lot of factories in the Soviet time. In my parents' time… Nothing was left after the Soviet Union disbanded.

Two years ago I brought my son here with me. My son was then ten years old. The idea was that he would stay with me. I wanted both to work and to care for my child. I couldn't do it, I could not. I was getting up at six in the morning and going to work. My son was left alone. Back then my sister was studying at college. I was leaving him with her. I was coming home at nine in the evening and still couldn't spend time with my child. I started working in a café so that I could have more time for my child. It didn't work out again. I was only getting 1500 Turkish Lira as a salary. That wasn't enough for my child, for me, for our transportation costs, for food and everything else. I couldn't sustain it. I didn't. I couldn't stay here with my son. I just had him here for two months, and then brought him back to Turkmenistan and came back here again.

I started babysitting again, as a *live-in* baby-sitter. That's good. You can earn more and spend less. But you're under psychological pressure. You're 24/7 under camera surveillance in someone's house. So you can't move around as you would like. It's a weird feeling. This is my only problem. Now there are cameras everywhere. It used to be different in the past, but now employers are installing them in their houses. In some rooms there are definitely cameras. In the child's room, the living room, the kitchen. But not in the parent's room, and not in my room. But of course, I would like to have it in my room, as well. Because the employers are talking so badly about babysitters, you know. That they beat the children or something like that. So, actually it's better to have cameras. I'm not against it at all. You're under pressure. You always need to keep an eye on things and don't feel comfortable. "Did I do something wrong here? Did I say something wrong?" You can't even talk on the phone.

---

1 Russian: Factories in USSR.

I have one day off. I leave the house for four days a month. I have rented an apartment, as well. All foreign babysitters and *live-in* housekeepers have already such an apartment they share together with three or four girls in a similar situation. They all share the rent. They meet there on weekends. First they go shopping and get whatever they want, and then cook and eat everything together at home. They also have breakfast the next morning and then leave for work. I usually go straight home and sleep. In the afternoon, my sister joins me. She's a babysitter, too. My other sister is studying at college. We cook at home and then we walk around the mall. Sometimes we go out to the park and train.

Internet connections are everywhere now. So everybody is using it.

There are apps. We use *Line.* I'm usually using it to make a phone or video call. Every weekend I'm calling home on the landline. We talk by video-link, we talk on the phone. Sometimes I record my voice and send sound messages.

The other day, my son's cousin wrote me in the place of my son. I immediately sensed it. I said, "My son didn't write this." His cousin swore that he was my son. I said, "Okay, son, but don't swear again." But I know whom I'm writing to. I knew it wasn't my son. I felt it. Then I talked to my son and he didn't know anything about that chat. I think I just felt it. After all, I'm a mother... That's why I felt it.

We come here, work, and send money back home. We send it from here, they get it there. We have our own cargo companies. In Aksaray and in Laleli. I send money once in a month. I give $100 to a woman, for example. She takes this $100 and sends it over and then charges me $3 for the transfer. Probably the only thing that I haven't yet sent is a real house. I've sent everything else. Recently my son called me and ordered molasses. I said OK. An iPad, a bike, a scooter, I've sent everything to my son. I've sent him an iPad's twice in a year. I send the original chargers. He wants them. And not just one. "Send three or four." he says. "If one gets damaged, then I'll use the other one." So he substitutes my absence with this. He has a lot of wishes because I'm not there. I can't say no to his wishes. I can't say, "One charger is enough." Because I'm living apart from him. I can't say, "Use it carefully." I'm away. Every year I send him on holidays. I'm not there. He asks for it. I can't say "No." I wish I could refuse him but I can't. "My mother sent this, my mother sent that." The kids are showing off. "He's got that, mom, so please send the same to me." He's just a child. I think the child substitutes my absence with these things.

I used to miss him a lot. It was the first time we were separated. I even wrote a poem for him. But since I hadn't seen him for a long time, I get

used to it. I'm not the same anymore. Do you understand? When I came first –
of course, the child was small as well – I was having a hard time. I didn't care
about the money and I was thinking "I will go away." But what am I going to
do when I go back? I raised my child on boiled rice water until he was one year
old. And then, my mother said, "Enough is enough. Give me the child. Don't be
worrying yourself. I will take care of him; he's my precious one." A year later
she got cancer and passed away. My father had a heart attack twenty days after that and died. I had to leave my child with my sister. I couldn't move away
from here either. Those were distressing times. I couldn't go back. Now I'm
used to it. I don't want to go back now. I don't want to. I wish that my son would
grow up and come over here soon. I never want to go back again. Never ever.

I was always babysitting boys, for I'm a mother of a boy. I never
accepted girls. All the love that I couldn't give to my son I wanted to
give to those other kids. I can give it to these kids. I think my child is being
cared for in the same way that I care for these children. This is how I feel.

Whenever I get stuck into my job it takes my mind off him, but I never
completely forget him for a single day. Whenever I open my eyes in
the morning, I remember my son. At night when I put my head on the pillow,
I remember him. I pray to Allah, that it is over soon. Sometimes I'm counting
the days. With each passing day I'm getting closer to my son. Oh, I'm getting
closer to him. I say "Yet another day."

I worry if someone might get angry and beat my son and he wouldn't
tell me about it. I mean, I have this fear that my child is sad and he
doesn't tell me or can't tell me about his feelings. This is my fear, nothing else.
For example, he sees some parents fondling their child or something. My son
would see that and feel sad. But he wouldn't tell me that. He would hide this
from me. I think he'll hide it. My son probably knows it. His mother is there
and she will come back one day. Whenever I call him he says "Mama, I miss
you". He wants to know, when I will come back and take him. ▬

"I never expected her to bring me presents or anything but I did expect her to talk to me more and to have a mother-daughter relationship."

Lenuţa Alţâna, Romania

My name is Lenuţa and I'm 15 years old. I was born in Maramureş.

My mother was married to… someone… They got married and then separated. They did not stay together for long. My mother left me with my grandparents in Maramureş. Then she went to Germany and got married to someone else. Then, when I was four, she took me to her husband in Craiova, where I stayed with her until I got to third grade. Then she went back to Germany. After that they no longer stayed in contact with each other. I stayed there with my stepfather. I was fine. He treated me well and even took me to school. We got along well. I stayed there until I was in fifth grade. Then I came here to live with my aunt.

All I know about my mother is that she's working in a restaurant, or a kind of bar. We don't talk too much about it, but she said she works in Mannheim.

I never expected her to bring me presents or anything but I did expect her to talk to me more and to have a mother-daughter relationship. But she avoids me and my questions. She also has a relationship, but she doesn't want to admit it. In the three weeks she was here in the summer, we didn't do anything together.

I wouldn't like to move in with my mother, not really … no. As she behaves now, I don't want to. If my mother came back, she would have to give him up, so I don't want my mother to have a relationship with that guy there. But I'm helpless; I just can't do anything. If she came back, he couldn't come. I told her: "It's him or me." As you can see, she chose him.

Before that she was not like that. Since she went to Germany she's become like that. Well, I can't say for sure that she doesn't miss me, but if she really did, she would give anything to see me more often.

Nevertheless, what I wish for most is that she would be with me. One would have to change the situation in Romania so that, for example, parents could come back and find a job. Not necessarily in the city or something, but that they should be with their children. We could lead a modest life; you do not always need to live in luxury, right? That's my opinion. Or the parents should at least take their children with them abroad.

But sometimes I think maybe it's too complicated for parents to have children, maybe they just don't want them. I'm sure it's hard to have children, educate them, bring them to school. Sometimes it might be easier for parents to be alone without children.

There are certainly many other children with this problem. But I don't know anyone who feels this way and with whom I could talk about it.–

"I needed all these years to work to provide them with the money they needed. To make my daughter finish school and now her studies."

Barbara Istanbul, Turkey

Back then, my children were in high school. We were in the middle of paying their expenses for their education. I'm the one who is helping them with their education, for their father couldn't help them. So, then I decided to go abroad because my ... my husband's salary wasn't enough to raise the kids. I decided to try Taiwan, London, but my destiny, my destination was here, in Turkey. I've been here for almost ten and a half years without going back.

So I needed all these years to work to provide them with the money they needed. To make my daughter finish school and now her studies. It's just ... my husband is ... I removed him from my life. I was fed up. I earn money to save money. But nothing. For ten years, instead of investing the money he earned, he was always gambling and drinking. My eldest son has his own family already. He has two kids and he didn't finish his university. But, I hope he will go to Japan to work in October. So at least he can finally raise his own family. My youngest son is the one who is taking care of our business. I always trust him. He's the one who is handling it. He is like the father of the family now. He's taking care of his elder siblings. It's a big relief for me to have somebody to help raise the family.

They say I am very strong. I miss my mom. Even my grandchildren, I didn't see them. I miss them. I'm still praying.

I'm still hoping that I can arrange to sort out my papers one day so that at least I can go, go back home. When I came here my visa was like a transit visa. A formality they said, it's just a transit visa. I used to go to Cyprus. But it was just a formality. My real destination was Istanbul. One can only stay there seven days and then one has to exit, but I didn't leave. I stayed here. To be able to remain here legally, you have to marry somebody and then after three years or more you can separate from him. I had a fake marriage so as just to have the papers. I just shook hands with the man, a sixty-one year old man and then nothing. I never saw him again. I just got the papers. My employer paid for the marriage. They had to pay for that. I didn't pay anything because we had an agreement. But officials investigated and said: "We have investigated and asked his neighbors and at the market in his neighborhood, and they don't know you." So I was to become illegal again.

Even though I don't have papers I'm lucky in that I've always found good employers. I've been here almost eleven years and I already have had three employers, and this is my fourth. I'm lucky that they are good families. I enjoy taking care of the kids. They treat me like family. And all my employers have always been my friends. The babies I once took care of, they're growing up now. They send me messages like: "I love you, I miss you."

I have family here. My sister and my niece are here as well. They also live in Istanbul but we don't all have the same day off. Her day off is Wednesday so unfortunately we can only see each other once every two months... but we chat on the phone and so on.

Maybe the only thing that makes me strong here is my faith. I'm closely connected with my sisters here in the church. We meet here in the Legion of Mary meeting at church. The faith, my faith here, this is like a real family in this community. So that's why I feel strong. That is my life here.

I will go home. Let's see, maybe in two years time. Maybe in the near future, if my business is stable and my son is also stable in his job and my daughter graduates and finds herself a job. Maybe I could return home, to be with them and with my mother. I miss my mother of course... But I don't know what my life will be like if I go back home forever... Hopefully, my employer can arrange my papers, so that I can visit my family, go there, and come back here. That is what I'm praying for.

So I hope the business I've just started with my youngest son in the Philippines will work out. We started a quail farming business. It's like a poultry farm. It's a good business. Unlike hens, quails lay eggs twice a day. We have more than five thousand quails. We should collect 8000 eggs per day. 5100 quails are growing now and laying eggs. This is a good income. That's why I decided to start this business. If it succeeds I will save some money, expand it, and make it bigger. I hope it will succeed. I hope next year it will be easier for me. I am just starting. This year is a bit shaky, but next year I hope all will be fine, and that business will settle down. I hope so.

My son is sending me photos. He is constantly in contact with me.

Because the Internet is in the backyard, he takes photos and then sends them to me. I've also asked him to take photos of the eggs. He's the one taking care of business. Though the youngest he's the one who is a father to my other kids. There is a cycle. The bird lays eggs for only one and a half years. After that you can sell the birds as meat, as chicken. You can sell it and then you can order another set of chicks and then the cycle begins over again. So there's no losing of money. I'm really happy that we've started making money. If the business succeeds, my son also wants to expand.

But they're still relying on my salary. They are waiting on it. That's what my salary is for. I get it and then "puff." Nothing. Nothing left for me. I send it all to them. My husband...(*laughing*) I don't trust him with money. I transfer money to my son. But he has even fooled my son, too. He said that he would order some steel because it's cheaper. Later on we found out he hadn't ordered anything. He just gambled the money away. So, I said, "that's enough." I spoke with my son, "Okay, you can continue that business, but your dad can have no part of it. He won't do anything."

He is still their father, but they understand me. I kicked him out of my house. He now lives in his grandmother's house. Even he tried to persuade my son to talk to me, so as to accept him back again. But I refused and told them to tell him to speak with me directly, if he wanted. He's afraid to talk to me.

Maybe if my husband hadn't been like this, I wouldn't have gone abroad. But somebody has to care for the business and somebody has to take care of the family. ▬

**"I was ready to go back to Ghana, when I
realized I was pregnant. It was not love that
made me stay in Germany. It was the baby."**

Afia Berlin, Germany

And I didn't want to have an abortion. I feel that an abortion wasn't right. If I had decided to go back to Ghana when pregnant, the fate of the new-born wouldn't have been good. It would mean a kind of "generational suffering." The child's father has a German passport because he has been here for more than thirty years. His children are German. So I called my eldest daughter in Ghana and said: "Listen, this is the situation: You've always been crying out for a brother or a sister. You're going to get one. But I can't come now. I first need to have the baby. And then I will come and get you. So then we all can live together. I know it isn't easy living with somebody else. Hang in there, I'm coming soon." But it didn't happen.

She was ten years old then, still a child. She was missing her mother. She was crying. She complained "why?" Because she and I were alone. It was always only just the two of us. We had done everything together... You would always see her with me. Just like my handbag. Always happy. And all of a sudden this situation.

Now she is fifteen and basically lives in a boarding school because there's no one to take care of her. My mother lives really far away in a village. And she can't stay with her. So my daughter lives in school. At first she was staying with a friend and his wife and I was sending money for food and everything at the end of every month. Because she was eating in their house, using electricity. So I sent them money for her upkeep. But I didn't realize, that when the husband was out at work, his wife was mal-treating my child... She has a mark on her leg from a beating she received from the woman. So that's why I moved her out of there and took her to the school. But whenever the school is closed on vacation, her accommodation becomes a problem. So, she ends up moving from one place to another.

And she feels she's been neglected and that I don't love her, because I have two other children here. That's how she feels. Because, I don't get her everything she asks for. Because I don't have the money. I pay her fees, I buy her clothes, I buy... whenever she asks for something she has to buy; provisions, a little, little food and sugar and things she likes to eat. Something you don't have to cook but you can just eat straightaway, things like that, provisions. She has to buy all of them and it is very expensive in Ghana. It costs the same money. I have to pay fees. Transport.

Everything. And knowing she's not really living with somebody…

Somebody I can trust. Nobody cares about her.

I went to see this lawyer. He knows it isn't easy and he told me that if I could find at least four-hours work with a contract, then he could fight for me to have her brought here. Sometimes I go to the *Jugendamt*[1] and they say: "What? Why don't you bring her here?" Because I can't. Nothing. There is no law protecting that child there. Yes, they said, if I'm not working here, then I cannot bring her. It means that whenever I bring her here, I have to take care of her. So, it's not possible. I think the government should realize… Because there is no German mother who lives in one place but her child lives somewhere else, no.

Sometimes I sit on that couch and my mind is absent. That is what is eating me up because I see the mistake my cousin made by not bringing her older son here. I might be making the same mistake. Do I go back with my children to Africa? Do I stay here with my children? Everything is messed up in my head. I don't know what to do. That's why I went to seek help from the *Jugendamt*. Because I was going crazy. I was always sitting here, crying. Because I was confused. I don't know what to do. I don't know who to approach, who to talk to.

Whenever I want to eat with my kids, I think about her "Is she eating? What is she eating? Is she OK?" As these questions pop up, I lose my appetite… So I always play some music. Something to distract me from thinking. So I always play some music and dance to it.

These two other children are from the same father. I don't want them to look down on her. She is my first child. They will come to know her as their big sister. "Even though we're not from the same father, she is our big sister." And then they will love her as a sister. They will not only see her as a sister, but there will be love. That feeling, you feel for your sister, will be there. —

1 German: Youth Welfare Office.

"Nobody knew that I was leaving at three o'clock in the morning. Her grandmother was sleeping next to my youngest daughter, they were all asleep. So I left."

Munisa Istanbul, Turkey

It's been a year now since I came to Turkey. I came alone. I knew no one, I know no one. I'm married and I have three children. I have to take care of them. I had to do something so I borrowed the money, bought the tickets and came here. I'm working here. I send the money back to my family in Uzbekistan. That's how I take care of my three children.

I arrived at Istanbul airport. I had no one. I didn't know the language, I knew nothing. A girl collected me; she's also one of us, an Uzbek. We stayed in a hotel, the two of us, two women. After running out of money, what could we do? No job, without anybody. Then I found Rosa, this "mother" of mine. She took me to her home. I stayed at her place for a while. She found me a job. Got my residency permit done. She helped me with all sort of things.

I worked at a house. Then at a hospital. I was taking care of an old lady. Then I quit. I went back to my hometown, because I missed my kids a lot. I couldn't stand it, that's why. Our country, it is beautiful; it's very calm, but there are no jobs.

My youngest daughter... she is ten years old; she was nine when I left. She was sleeping. I left at three o'clock in the morning. She woke up next morning, but her mom isn't there. They told me she had cried a lot, for I had left without saying goodbye. Nobody knew that I was leaving at three o'clock in the morning. Her grandmother was sleeping next to her [my youngest daughter], they were all fast asleep. So I left.

They can take care of themselves. They say "We're not children anymore." My eldest daughter looks after the household. Where I come from, a child can do anything at ten years old. My daughter cooks, irons. She deals with everything. Her father does nothing. She comes from school, takes care of her father, feeds him, and does the ironing. She does the laundry, cleans the house. Aside from all that, she also goes to school. But my youngest daughter, she gets mad and becomes sad. I feel miserable. She says: "Don't go. Please work here, don't go; if not, take me with you." That's why it's so hard for me. That's why I cannot look after children. I don't want to baby-sit. Because once I see kids, I won't be able to take it.

I contact home via WhatsApp, Telegram, Imo. We talk. But I don't talk to them on the phone so much. I don't talk much. Any time I call them, it's their father who picks up the phone. I don't want to talk with him; I want to talk with my children. That's why I don't talk much on the phone.

My daughter calls, whenever she needs something, or whenever she misses me. She calls me in the evenings and asks, "Are you free, can we talk?" but I can't talk much. I don't know why, but my eyes fill with tears. That's why I cannot stand it. Sometimes I say, "OK I'm busy now, but I will call you later." Sometimes I don't even want to talk.

Sometimes they get sick and I call and tell them "Go to a doctor, take this or that medicine, get a good rest, or don't go to school!" Their father wouldn't know what to do. I explain what they have to do. Fathers don't know how to take care of children. No, it's not a usual thing amongst us. They only ask: "Where are you going? Where are you coming from? Is dinner ready?" It is how they look at fatherhood. I've to work. If the father doesn't take care of the children, I can. At least one person should work in this family, right?

I always ship packages. Once a month. Food would stick in my throat if they don't have something to eat. Chocolate, cheese, clothes…I send them everything. I ship everything from here. She waits for the package, and asks, "Did you send it? When is it going to arrive?" Sometimes they receive it five days later, sometimes ten days later. I also send money, in dollars. They change the money there and spend it. It's meant for school expenses and shopping for the house.

My younger daughter took my pyjama and stuffed it with something that made it look like me. You see? And she also put a pillow underneath it. My elder daughter was so scared when she saw it. She said, "For an instant I thought you were lying there." She [my younger daughter] cuddled it and slept like this. She says, "I did not wash [the pyjama] because it smells like you." She was up all night, crying. My elder daughter says, "Mom, she's going crazy."

My kids say, "It would also be fine if you don't work, money doesn't matter; just stay here, don't go!" I ask them: "What do you need from here? Whatever you need, I can send it from here. Do you need any money? What would you like?" They want nothing at all. You know if you ask children whether they want something, then they tell you. But mine don't. They only say: " We don't need a thing, only you, come and don't go back." But I went back home and stayed for two months. I couldn't take care of them while I was there. What can I do? There was no work. I went there, how many times, no work! Even if there was… let me put it this way: The salary is around fifty or eighty US dollars. I couldn't afford to take care of them. How could I? I have three kids and a sick husband. How can I take care of them? I explained them the situation to them. Here, I earn at least 500 US dollars. Then they said: "OK, go to work and earn some money so that you can come home sooner."

I like myself a lot. That's why I groom myself. When I set my profile picture in WhatsApp, my boss told me to remove it. He said: "Please delete this." If I said "no", then he would say, "If anyone saw this photo, they would not hire you." How would I know? So, I deleted it. I just put a random picture as my profile picture. Not my picture. He said, "Now, tie your hair up, dress properly, and trim your nails." I said, "My nails are not that long to cut anyway." He said. "Don't wear too much make-up." I said "OK."

I don't like Laleli. It's too crowded. But the shipping company is there.

That's why I go there. I enjoy the seaside. I like calm places. Whenever we meet, we go somewhere to eat Uzbek food. We hang out at a mall, or go to the seaside. Afterwards everybody goes back home or to work. We don't always go to Laleli. We go there out of necessity. We ship our packages; we have a bite to eat, and then leave. ▬

"We worked things out ... we tried to function. I'm very proud of my kids; we trust each other and always work like good colleagues, like friends."

Irma Berlin, Germany

My decision was that I had to go. Definitely. There was no perspective in Bosnia. And I've often thought about it, but the war has been over for twenty years now and the situation has not improved. There is a very bad political and social situation there. There is a lot of crime, corruption, and I don't like all that combined. Because of my children and their future, their lives. In Bosnia, there is no positive feeling for the future. You can't plan life. Also, financially, my salary was 200 Euro, but prices are the same as in Germany. One can imagine how this money can't be enough. And especially as a single mother with two children who are going to school and need a lot of things. I've decided to go.

I also talked to the kids back then; they were still kids, but I can talk to them just like they were adults. We decided together that it would be better that I leave. But I didn't know that everything would be so hard. And of course to start a life, all over again from the beginning. It was hard. I'm forty-eight years old - I need a bit of rest, to enjoy life for a bit and so on, but it doesn't work out. That is hard. I used to say that you have to be patient, you have to keep going, you have to bring your kids someday. I have been here for about a year and four months. I am a licensed nurse but currently I'm working as a nursing aid until my diplomas are recognized.

In the beginning I had no phone, no Internet and we couldn't communicate much. It was very difficult and sad. The children were alone at home. I've been living separately from my husband for eight years. The children were alone in the apartment. My daughter is eighteen years old and my son fourteen. They were not adults yet. And they had to buy everything themselves, to cook for themselves and everything. Now my daughter told me the apartment was a disaster, but back then she told me, "Mom, everything is fine, don't worry, we've got something to eat, everything is fine." And my son said the same. I knew that with the food, it wasn't okay. She can't cook. Every week I put together a package and sent it to Bosnia by bus. There were different things in it. Mostly sweets, and for Jelena clothes. She likes that. During this period, I lost about eleven kilos.

In the beginning I didn't have internet at home, but I found a place where there was a connection. How often I stood in this building, and telephoned. Yes, that was sad. Sometimes at half past four in the morning in the winter on the street …"Hello, how are you, all right?" And then, after work at three o'clock. …"Hello?" But okay…We… we probably tried to solve the problems, so we always tried to have fun. Our conversations were funny, always comical, and a bit playful. I always tried, and they too also tried to be funny. They did that because of me and I did it because of the kids. It was only after I hung up that I was sad and asked myself, what am I doing here? Is this all right? We worked things out … we tried to function. I'm very proud of my kids; we trust each other and always work like good colleagues, like friends.

But I always remained positive. I thought depression was a luxury. I couldn't afford that. I have to be strong. But I'm not strong. I am sensitive, emotional, very much so. It's time for me to fix everything, and then I can be like I was before. A woman, a sensitive, emotional woman. I like to read books, I like to go for a walk, I like movies, art, but for many years I haven't been able to afford such things. They're luxuries for me. Now I have to fight. Now I am a fighter. But I hope only for a short while.

At home, I found a solution. I studied a lot. I was convinced that I had to learn German. I have to learn, that could be useful. I haven't seen a movie in three years. That's my passion. But that doesn't work. Nevertheless, I don't think negative things… I always try not to do so. That doesn't help. I always say, "thank God." What's done is done. I get on with it and I have my dreams. I like travelling. Small cities, lots of sun, cafes, peace, my books, theatre, cinema … and sometimes to travel. This is my dream… We enjoy little things. ▬

"… we talk by phone five or six times a day. I can't make it if I don't."

Andra Sibiu, Romania

I first went to Italy because I had a son and I had I tried to let him grow up with the money I could have earned here I wouldn't have succeeded. He was six, seven, small, very small, it was heavy, very heavy. I cried all the way to Italy the first time I left.… Besides my son, of course, my parents were also a reason. I also helped them with the money.

The first time I left, I stayed longer. I did not come back home immediately. At that time, we also needed a visa, that was much more difficult, we were not yet in the EU.

In the beginning I worked without a contract, without anything, in a place in the mountains in a factory for making resin glass. We lived in a kind of caravan. It had two rooms and a kitchen. We were five or six, all Romanians. There was no room for a child. I worked all day long, with a break for lunch and a break for dinner, so we stopped at nine in the evening. But we didn't even have time to cook something; we never had time … One could not have brought a child, absolutely not. I remember well, this first time. Although I've tried to forget those times, I remember them only too well and they weren't very nice.

Now I've found another job. Let's say I'm fine. I work for three or four months and then return back home for three months. So, I also have time to be at home with my son. Of course, my absence still upsets him. Well, now he's got used to it a bit and he also knows that there are only a couple of months until I return again. And we talk by phone five or six times a day. I can't make it if I don't … at night I have to … Thankfully, there are phones. If they didn't exist, I wouldn't be able to make it. So we're more in touch, and if I have to hear his voice at twelve o'clock at night; then I'll put my hands on the phone and call him and he knows he has to answer me… always… and he'll answer me any time! … If not, I can't sleep.

In the past, at my first job, I could only make phone calls once a day, from the landline phone. There was a landline phone in the house, so it was like being in jail (laughs). Back then he didn't talk to me that way, he was small then… yes, it was much harder. Today it's better. I hear him, I hear how he's doing, I know every day what he's doing … what his worries are.

Again and again he sends me these video messages that you find on Facebook. With mom without mom, different variants, these short videos, with food, with what he wants to eat, so then he sends me some recipe that I should cook when I get home. Or he films the apartment and compares when Mom is at home and when she's away. All the clothes are fine, and then when Mom isn't there, everything is a mess ... (*laughs*) A clutter. Something like that. So that makes me ... I'm deeply saddened whenever he sends me these messages. And I feel that I miss him. That's not ... Yes, that's tough anyway. ... because I'm not there, with him. I suffer many pangs of conscience.

In certain things he's more attached to my mother than to me ...

because he has spent so much time with her. Because she practically raised him. They are very close. She may understand him a bit better than I do ... I don't know ... Sometimes that makes me a bit jealous because then I think (*laughs*) that he's a bit closer to my mother than to me ... Yes.

One of my friends brought her child with her. He was older and she

did not succeed in integrating him. No, because, children are a bit vicious and don't easily accept foreign children. Probably, if you bring a child from childhood on, when it's very small and that it learns to speak, it is different. But, if it is already big, it is much more difficult. I was scared that something might happen to him ... yes ... that he could not ... integrate himself. So for his mental health... I was also afraid. That would have been such a strong disillusionment ... yes ... I don't know. I didn't want to let him hang around. Besides, I was always working, I was alone, and how could I have managed that? Who would have stayed with him then? I would then have to rent somewhere, and then I would have had no money left to survive. And then, when he was older, he didn't want to come anymore. He has also found more and more friends here in Romania. His life is here. Who is to blame for the fact that I had to leave? Whose fault? ... I can't say exactly ... On the whole, I left to earn the money to feed and to raise my son. ▬

"I've never reproached my mom for what she actually did to us. There is a lot of unsaids about everything that happened."

Tülay Munich, Germany

I was born in 1980 in Şereflikoçhisar, a small town near Ankara. My dad came to Germany in the late sixties, early seventies. He has been here for a very long time. My mom did not follow him until 1978, without us. I came to Germany at the age of nine. We are three siblings. I am the eldest, my sister, the middle one, my brother is the youngest. She took the youngest with her at the time. My brother was two years old then. My sister and I remained behind in Turkey. There used to be problems about family reunification; that's why they decided that mum would first come to Germany with the youngest. My father was supposed to ensure that we would also follow them as soon as possible. The whole thing took but two years. We didn't see my mom during these two years. We had no relationship with my father anyway. I first met my father when I was five. I thus lacked any connection to him. But, that mom had left us, that was painful. I was seven and my sister was three when we were left behind. During this period we hopped from one family to the next. Originally, we were supposed to stay with grandma, but she natuarally couldn't do much with two small children. She handed us over relatively quickly to other family members. From uncles to aunts, until we had passed through the paternal side. Then we were passed over to the maternal side. We traveled around within the family.

Once I came home from school, it was autumn or winter, really icy cold. There, on the doorstep, was my little three year old sister, in her underwear and pyjamas with three bags crammed with our things. The little girl came running up to me and I asked, "What's up?" My cousin flung open the door and said "Take your things, and your sister and piss off!" Years later I learned that my father didn't seem to have paid the promised child allowance on time. That's why they simply kicked us out on the streets. That was quite a formative experience for me. So much for family love.

During holidays, the children's parents would return to Turkey – mostly just their fathers. There were two children, there were only the fathers in Germany and there were two children, who were just getting along like me. We used to ask each other, "What did you get, what did they bring you," but we would never ask, "aren't you feeling good" or something in that line. I remember keeping a diary. That's where I always wrote about who I was angry with. My cousin found it one day and I got a beating. What a real shame that it was taken from me and destroyed. I think that it would have told volumes. Were it possible, I'd love to read what I had written in it as a nine-year-old.

Then we came to Germany. It wasn't a problem for me at all, but it was very, very hard for my sister. For a long time she refused to call my mom "mom." As far as my sister was concerned, I was always "mom." That hurt my mom a lot. Perhaps that might have made her realize for the first time the consequences of this separation. She had to struggle for a very long time.

My mother says, "What should I have done, I was only allowed to take one child with me, so I took only one child, I was helpless." She presents herself as the victim. But I would have expected my mom to say that "either I take all my children or I won't come." She wasn't starving; we come from well-to-do families, she lacked for nothing, she lived in her own house, she had brothers around her who took care of everything.

When I look at my family in Turkey, they are always much better off than we are here. All the children were educated; they got everything they wanted. We had to work for everything. We had to struggle for everything. We were constantly being left completely alone. My mom left the house at half past five in the morning and didn't come back until seven in the evening. She had a bunch of keys with which she hurried from one cleaning job to the next, so that my father with his fat BMW could pretend in front of the family, what a great life we were having. She didn't even once bring us to school, she never even collected her children from the kindergarden, they never attended parents' evenings, nor celebrations, they neglected so much. For what? And now there's nothing left. We don't have any houses in Turkey, we have no shops. They've spent their lives here, risking so much, for damn all. That's not worth all the money in the world. So, I would've expected more that my mom would say "I can't bear to watch that my kids aren't feeling alright.' She used to telephone us so often, and I always told her, "Mom, come get us or come back to us." My daughter wouldn't need to tell me that twice ...

When I nowadays talk to my cousins or my youngest sister about those early day and she says, "can you remember that, then we were in this courtyard." Then that rattles me. But I completely repressed everything. I have vague memories about things. Nor can I remember the time I came to Germany, for the first one and a half years were a complete blank.

I got married at the age of sixteen. They probably thought "okay, they're developing too fast" and wanted to hit the brakes so to speak. I went on vacation to Turkey and came back married. To my cousin, my uncle's son. We had grown up together. We had slept together in a bed, we played together, we fooled around together, and now he was to be my husband? That was the awful thing for me, "he's just like a brother to me." They said they were doing something good because my uncle was pretty well-off. "It's just not supposed to be go outside, rather it's all supposed to stay in the family." That's really how it was a thousand years ago.

At that time, I felt abandoned and deceived for a second time. I could not accept it. Childhood memories resurged. "They're going to leave me in the lurch again." As a young girl you defend yourself against a whole horde of family members, but you haven't a chance. And then I understood, "keep your hands still, first do what needs to be done before there's no going back." I was terribly afraid that I would be sent back if I didn't do as I had been told.

I had started my training course and out of shame I told everybody there "No, I went down there, fell in love and got married." And so I was married for a quite a while. He wasn't allowed to enter Germany, for marriage by those under eighteen is not recognized here. But at some point the time came about. I had my training course behind me, and was of legal age. They then rented me a small apartment and he came to Germany. We realized relatively quickly "that it wasn't going to work out," and thank God we both saw it that way. I then decided to turn my back on the family and disappeard for a while. I couldn't see another way out.

Unfortunately, I lost track of my family. They abused me as a kid, they abused me as a teenager, and I didn't want to let them hurt me anymore. I can no longer accept anything, tolerate anything, respect anything that they thrust upon me. And that's exactly how it is for them. For them, I'm nothing and no one, for they see things differently. They no longer hold any esteem for me.

I haven't had any contact with my father since 2000. There has been some with my mom. Now that I'm a mother myself – I have a 10-year-old daughter – we're wrangling for the first time. Well, now the child in me, which thad been left behind all those years before, speaks up. I've never reproached my mom for what she actually did to us. There is a lot of unsaids about everything that happened. I thought I didn't want to hurt her; she certainly didn't do it on purpose, and she definitley had her reasons. But when my mom started criticizing me as a mother, everything in me erupted. Then

I thought, "You're not, don't you tell me what kind of a mother I am, you were never there for me, you left me behind, you kept me waiting, you made me suffer, you shoved me into the fire, the main thing was that the family was happy about it." These are things that erupted in me only after thirty years, and for the first time I had a broken relationship with my mother.

Our parents just missed out on so much and I can't understand the meaning behind it. I can't understand why. There's no reason on earth to leave a child behind. That's the crux of the matter that I'll never forgive. I will never show any understanding for it or tolerate it. I say that as a mom myself now, there's nowhere where I would go without my child, no matter what the circumstances. —

"Send me a pair of American jeans, if not –
you don't need to come."

Murat and his Family Audio Cassette, Eastern Turkey

Murat: We are recording this tape for you! Your son, Murat Metin on the 25.06.1976 at 15:11. Now we are sending you the tape recorded by your son Murat Metin. Now listen to the folk song that Murat Metin will present you. The first one is: *How Dark is my Destiny*

Murat: [singing] *How dark is my destiny! The sheep and its lamb aren't bleating together, Away from home, missing the mother, the father, the sister, and the brother, Where are my vineyards and orchards, my fragrant flowers, My vineyards and orchards, my vineyards and orchards, I cry and sigh away from home. I cry, I cry ahhh!*

Grandmother: Emine, how are you, what are you doing? I salute and kiss your and Hasan's eyes. I kiss Seda, Selda, Yonca and Semiha's eyes. My daughter, I pray for you five times a day. I sent you some pastry, some grapes and some walnuts. If you want to know more about Murat, he is very well and happy.

Older Cousin: Aunt! I am Yusuf. Listen! Send me a pair of American jeans, if not – you don't need to come. And also a vest. I wanted two. You prefer how many you will send, one or two. It is good if you send two. It is also good if you send one. In case you don't send any, you send a pair of jeans certainly. Don't forget, American jeans! I kiss your hands.

Younger Cousin: Emine Abla! Send me a train (*laughing*) with a key on it, but don't send anything for my older brother! (*laughing*) Emine abla, I wish God opens your way and you come here. I want also a pair of jeans, American jeans (*laughing*).

Older Cousin: Well done!

Younger Cousin: And a dress for my mother... a dress and also an airplane... An airplane, a train and a taxi, too.

Younger Brother: Bring everything... Then bring yourselves (*laughing*).

Grandmother: Emine, do not send any toys again. The children are not studying well. The toys have arrived today. I tell them to study. Whatever I say or do not say, they always play with them. Do not send any of them, OK? Do not send any toys to Ömer and Faruk.

Older Cousin: Emine Abla, don't worry about Murat, our grades at school are really good. We study our lessons. Don't worry. Maybe, there is only one bad grade or none at all. Do not worry about school, we are very good, we have everything.

Grandmother: Emine, your son Murat came today. I forgot to tell him: Do not send me anything! You sent clothes for your father. Doesn't he have clothes? Why did you send clothes? After your father came home in the evening, he called and and and went out with them. God knows, he loves and also. He loves them more than you do. Do not worry about them. Why do you always send something? Do not send me anything!

Murat: Mother! This is Murat. First, I greet you. I kiss yours and my father's hands. I also kiss my sisters eyes. I am very well. I missed you so much, you, and especially my sisters Seda and Selda. I always think of them. I am in a good mood. I'm very good here. They are taking good care of me here. How is my father? What is he doing? I greet him and respectfully kiss both his hands. I missed you so much. Mom! Record your voices on a tape and send it to us. I do not have anything else to say. I greet you again. I kiss yours and my father's hands. I kiss Yonca, Semiha, Seda and Selda's eyes.

Grandmother: Ömer, take it. You talk, too.

Younger Brother: Mom, I understood that I made a mistake, I said I kiss father Hasan's eyes. Well, that's wrong. I kiss his hands. I kiss Yasemin's hands too. I kiss Semiha, Seda and Selda's eyes. Do not worry about us, Mom. Me and Murat, we are so happy. Take care of yourselves.

Grandmother: Emine my dear, your tape player, I will sell it. I gave it to Ahmet and he took it to a guy. I said, "1500 liras". Ahmet bought a television, what will I do with a tape player? I will give it to anyone who buys it.

Emine! I missed you so much, I am worrying about you. How long will you stay there? What will happen later? I listened to Murat's tape. He sang folk songs. I cried. What's going on? What will happen to the kids? What a pity! They turned on the tape and I cried here. Now, you listen to the tape there and cry. What will happen? We are so sorry for you ... Well, you went away. God bless you. I hope Allah makes you return to your home. I hope Allah saves your children in that evil place and makes you come home. What should I do? Why don't you come back?

Aunt: Emine Abla, I am Fadime. I sold the dress and the shoes you gave me. I sold the shoes for 200 liras and the dress for 100 liras. I gave my father 300 liras, the trousers are left. I received your letter. I also received the goods you sent. You made us so happy. Thank you, Emine abla! We thank you so much! –

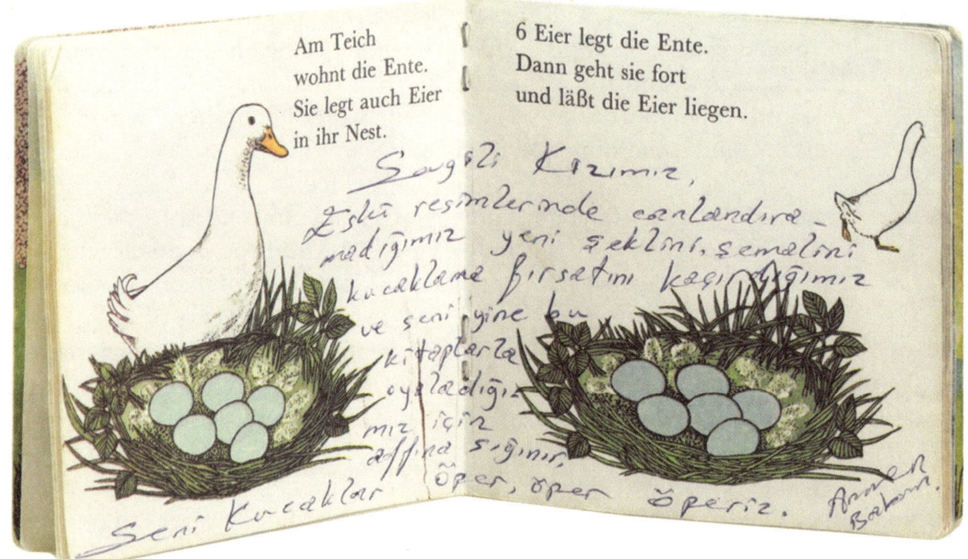

Picture book with dedication, Berna

Since birth, Berna has been cared for in Ankara by her grandparents, for her parents were working in Germany in the 1970s. Sometimes she came to Germany during holidays.
The book is a gift from her parents. The dedication reads: "Our dear daughter, we apologize to you for missing the opportunity to hug you – we can't imagine what you look like now from the old photos – and to have to comfort you once again with these books. Your Mom and Dad".

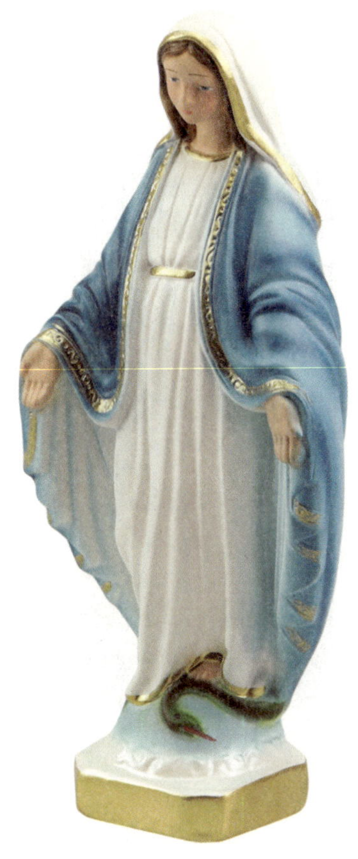

Holy Statue - Legion of Mary, Barbara

On Sundays, on their only day off, Filipino domestic workers congregate at the Catholic Church of St. Antoine in Istanbul. After the official service, they continue their prayers in a more intimate setting of the Legion of Mary. Here, between prayers, participants laugh, eat, and exchange news and worries. Sister Barbara says, "The faith, my faith here, is like a real family in this community. So that's why I feel strong."

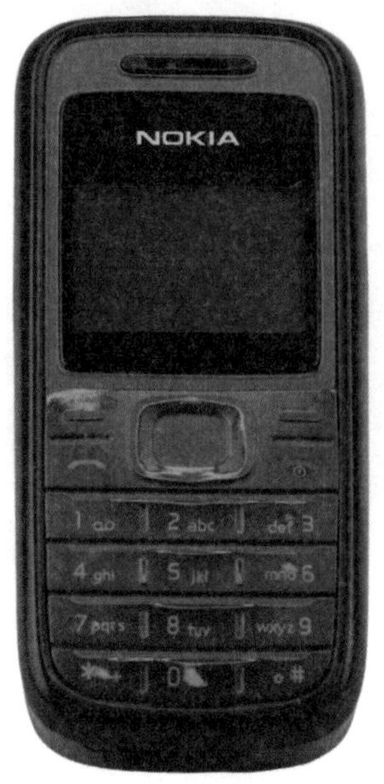

Nokia Mobile, Andra

Andra went abroad for the first time to work when her son was
ten years old. Today he is nineteen. In the beginning mobile
phones, later smartphones, and nowadays video-links have made
it easier for Andra to keep in touch with her son back in Romania.
They talk to each other five to ten times a day as well as at night.

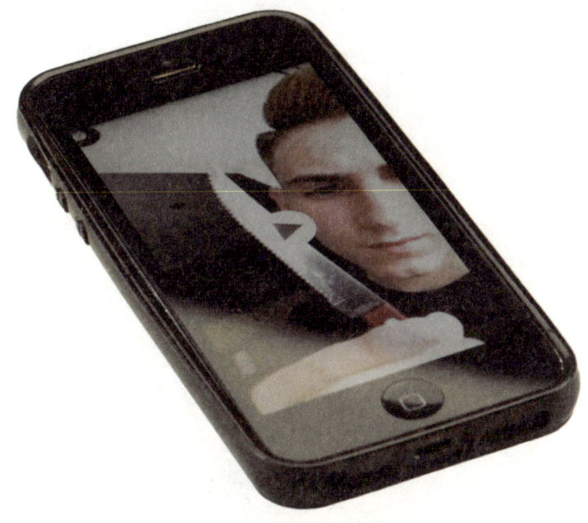

Smartphone with Video, Ionuţ

Ionuţ was left with his grandparents in the village when he was ten years old. His father disappeared immediately after his birth, so his mother had to travel to Italy to feed the child. Today, Ionuţ is nineteen. His mother is still travelling back and forth to Italy to work, but can return home more frequently, for Romania now belongs to the EU. In short videos, Ionuţ tells his mother about the lack of cleanliness and the reigning chaos at home while she is away.

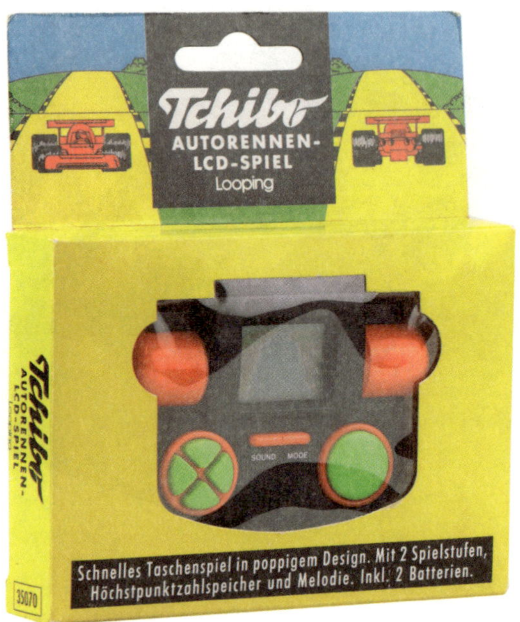

Pocket Game, Hasan

Every summer Hasan's parents came from Cologne to Turkey to visit their son.
For his sixth birthday, they brought him a pocket game with them. When they
returned for his seventh birthday the following summer, they again brought him
an identical pocket game, for they had forgotten the present they had brought
the previous year. Hasan never took the second gift out of its wrapping.

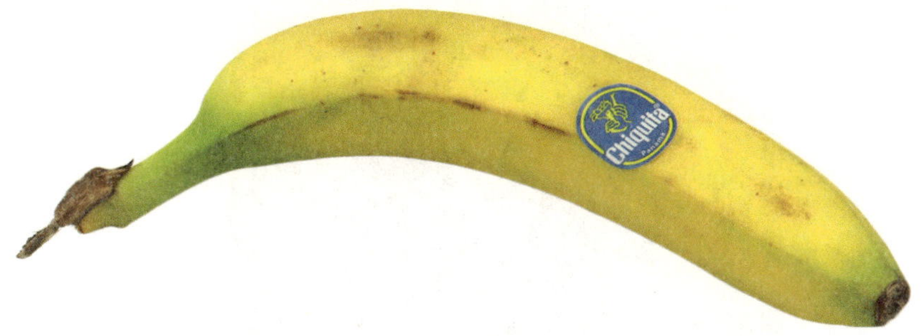

Banana, Eleni

Eleni's parents went to Germany as so-called guest workers. Eleni and her brother stayed with their grandparents in a small village behind Mount Olympus. The parents would send packages with clothes and sweets. In one package was a banana that Eleni ate proudly under the envious regard of other children in the village square.

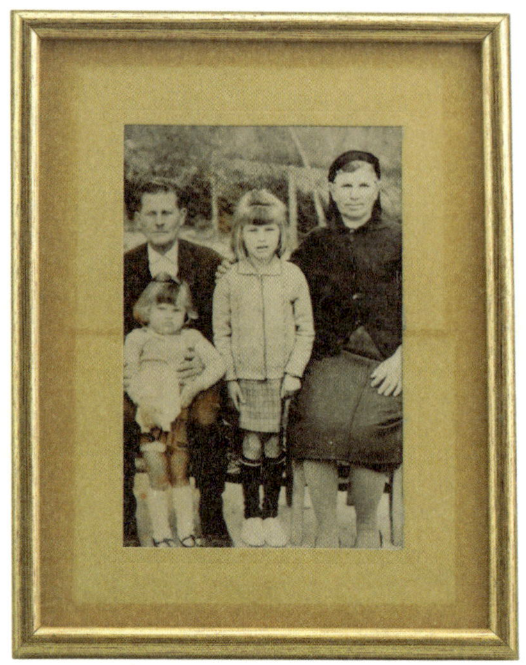

Photo with grandparents, Fotini

Fotini's parents travelled to Germany at the beginning of the 1970s
as so-called guest workers. Fotini suffered immensely from being
separated from her parents. The grandparents didn't get along with
the child, so the parents eventually had to be recalled from Germany.

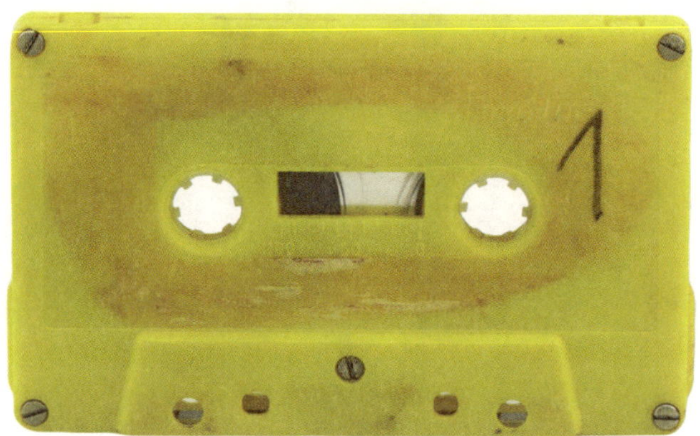

Audio Cassette, Murat

Murat was the only one of six siblings to grow up apart, at first with his grandmother in eastern Turkey and later with his uncle in Istanbul. He would sing songs and send them on cassette tape to the family in Germany. Other relatives in Turkey also raised their orders for dresses and luxury items on this cassette and informed Murat's parents about his life in the village. Murat was brought to Berlin at the age of sixteen only in 1981, because his parents were concerned that he might end up on the wrong track.

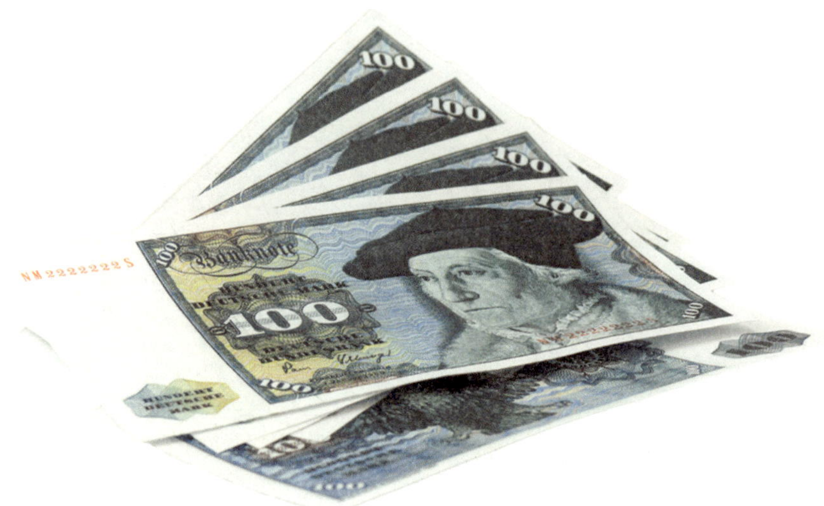

500 German Marks, Emine

Emine could not take all children with her to Germany. Her son grew
up separately from his siblings alone with his grandparents in Turkey.
Every time they went to visit Turkey her husband gave her 500 DM to
buy presents for their son.

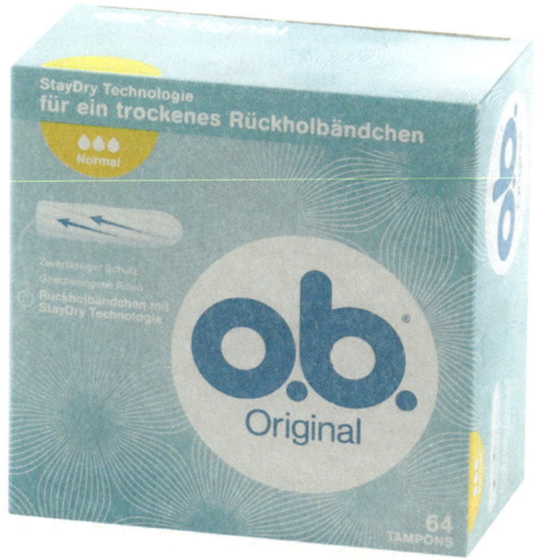

Sanitary Towels, Afia

For five years Afia's daughter has lived alone in Accra, Ghana, where she attends a boarding school. Afia can't bring her to Germany because of the immigration laws for family reunification. Now her daughter is in puberty and has started to menstruate. Such matters are difficult to discuss over the phone. Afia says there's no one around her daughter who can assist her concerning questions of growing up.

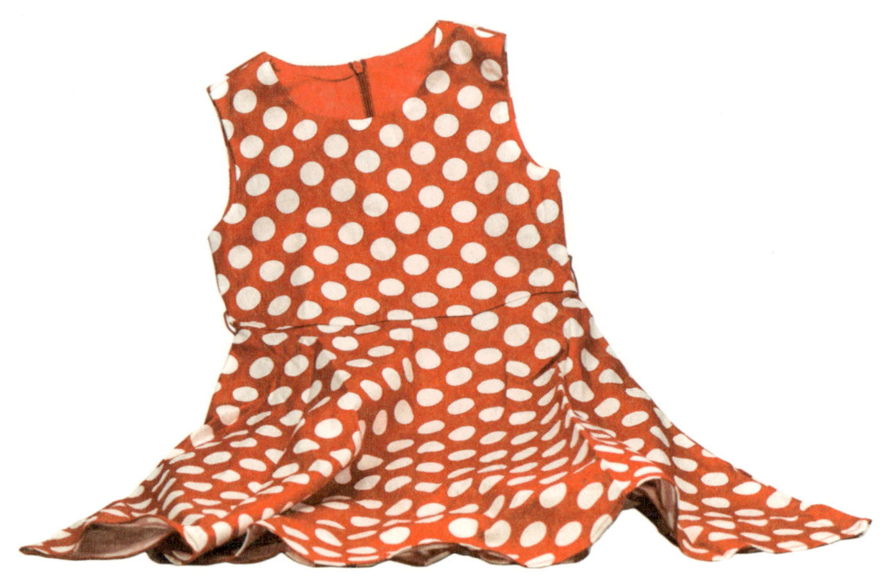

Cotton dress with red dots, Serpil

Almost every summer Serpil's father and stepmother came from Germany to the village. They brought gifts, but usually stayed only a few days before leaving without telling anyone. Once they brought this red dress with them. Serpil loved it more than anything else and washed it every time it got dirty so that she could put it back on immediately.

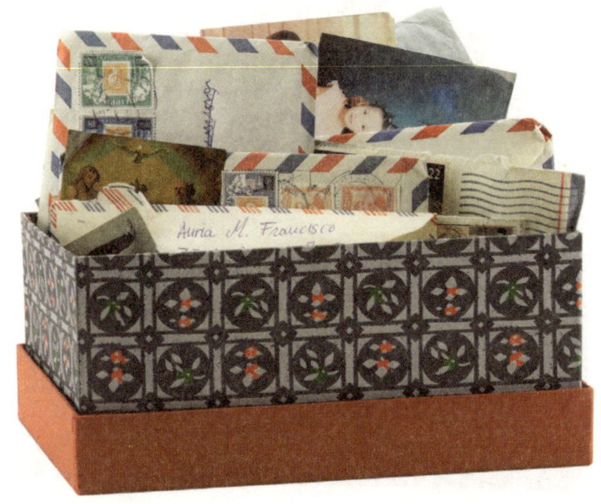

Box of letters, Angel

Before Angel left the Philippines eighteen years ago, her children gave her a letter on which was written on the envelope: "Dear Mom. But please don't read this in front of us. You have to read this in the airplane." Because her family is Catholic, they also placed a small cross inside the envelope. Angel keeps all the letters as well as the pictures and the clippings in a box. She is fond of keeping things.

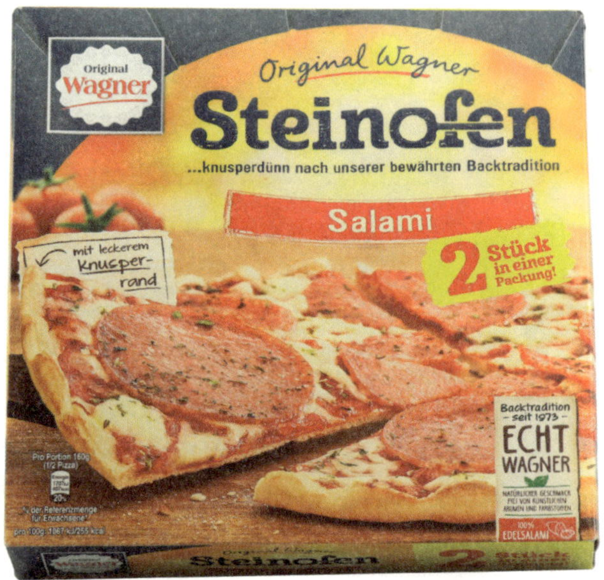

Frozen Pizza, Irma

Irma has been working as a nurse in Berlin since 2016. She had to leave her children behind in Bosnia. Irma worries about what her children eat when they are home alone because they can't cook. She has reduced her own life to a bare minimum and doesn't allow herself any treats.

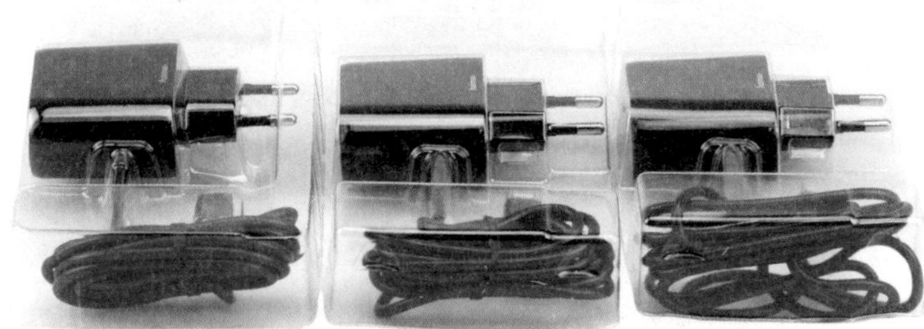

Smartphone Chargers, Gülnar

Gülnar left Turkmenistan because she was only able to feed her baby with cooking water from the rice pot. Her son is now ten years old and she has been unable to visit him for several years. Via video-telephone, he transmits his wishes to Gülnar that she should fulfill: for instance, a lot of smartphone chargers. Although his mother knows that he only needs one, she just can't say "no", for she can't be with him.

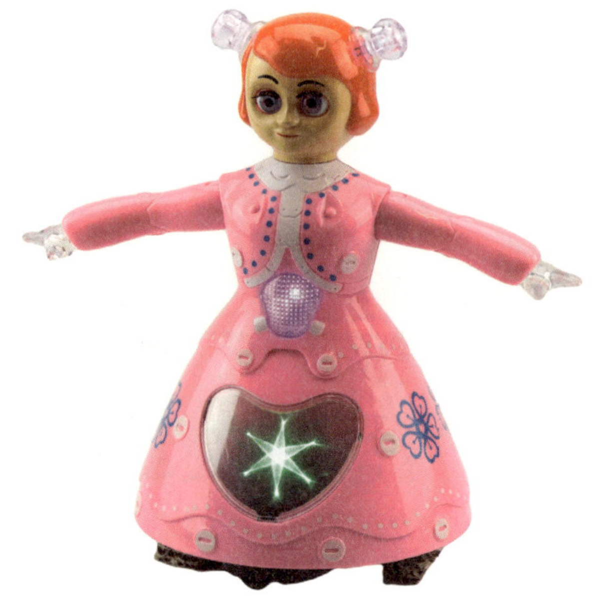

Dancing Doll, Lenuţa

Lenuţa's mother works in Mannheim. Lenuţa doesn't know where exactly. Once she brought a doll about which Lenuţa doesn't exactly remember. She never expected her mother to bring her presents. She longs that her mother stays with her and talks with her when she comes, so that they might have real mother-daughter relationship.

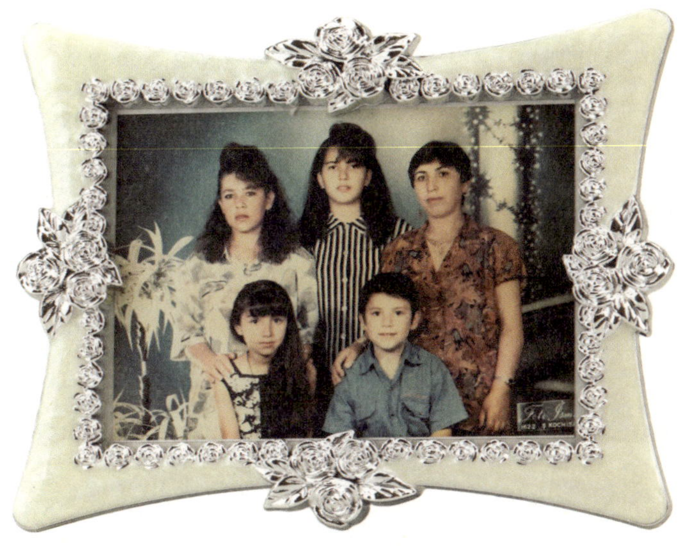

Family photo without father, Tülay

Tülay and her sister were left behind with various relatives in Turkey. Only at the age of nine was she brought to Germany. At sixteen, she was married to her cousin. Afraid of being sent back to Turkey, she accepted everything, silently. Later, she broke off contact with her father. Her relationship with her mother is difficult, for she herself now has a daughter.

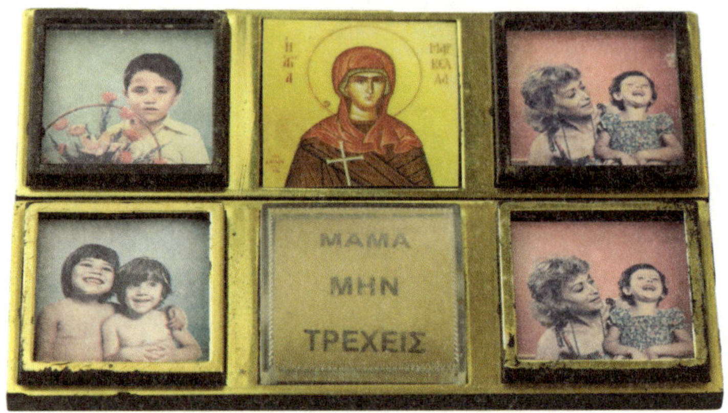

Magnetic Picture "Mama do not run," Anastasia

In 1969, Anastasia made her first journey from Chios to Germany. Her children remained in the care of her sister. They could soon buy their first car from the savings, with which they finally drove back to Greece so as to meet the children. The magnetic picture they put in the car after the vacation was to remind them of their children. After the first corner, she said to her husband, "Let's turn back!" But they didn't turn back.

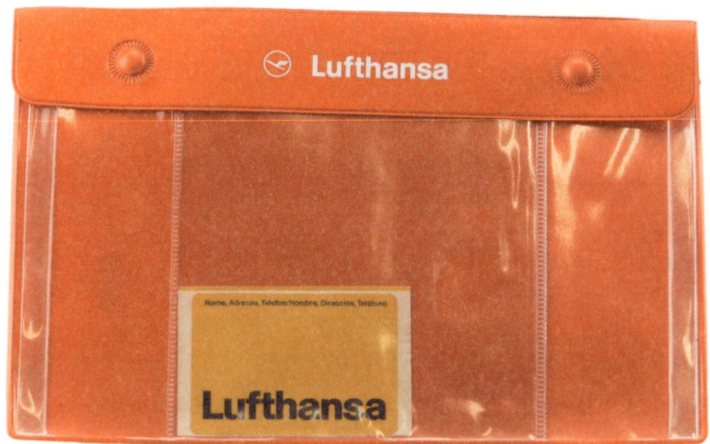

Lufthansa bag, Esra

The eight-year-old Esra kept her travel documents in this bag when she first traveled by plane to Germany with her parents in 1980. Her flight from Ankara to Dusseldorf made a stopover at Munich Airport. The flight was costly, but the airline offered flight accompaniment for children on request.

Glossary

Almancı	Designates people from Turkey living in Germany. Applied by Turkish citizens in Turkey, the term has derogatory overtones.
Balikbayan Boxes	(Tagalog: repatriate boxes) contain presents sent by overseas Filipino workers to their families and friends back home. The sending of *balikbayan boxes* was made tax-free by the Filipino government in 1987 so as to support the local population through remittances.
Brain Drain	Emigration of highly qualified workers or academics.
Care Chain	Coined by Arlie Hochschild (2000), the term describes the care deficit created by migrant women hired in the care sector as a loss for their children left behind. Their absence needs to be compensated for by family members or paid on-the-spot nurses.
Care Drain	A form of **Brain Drain**, denoting medical and care workers.
Chain Migration	Migrants tend to migrate to places, where they already know someone and can start more easily. Chain migration refers to migration to a particular place as a result of former migration to the same place.
Euro Orphans	Denotes children, who have at least one parent working in an other European country. The term refers to the easier and increased labor migration within the European Union.
Strawberry Orphans	Denotes children of seasonal workers who work abroad; it is also a synonym for Euro Orphan.
Gagauz	**Gagauz**, **Gagauz Yeri**, or **Gagauziya** is an autonomous region in the Republic of Moldova. The *Gagauz* language is a Turkic language, one reason why Turkey has proven to be an attractive destination for *Gagauz* migrant workers following the collapse of the Soviet Union.
Gastarbeiter	(German, lit. guest worker) the term *Gastarbeiter* took root in the 1960s in relation to workers who came to the Federal Republic of Germany in the wake of the recruitment agreements. For a long time it was assumed that they, like guests, would merely stay for a short period before returning to their home countries.

Pasalubong From Tagalog, "[something] for when you welcome me." In the Philippines it is common to bring presents from overseas for friends and family staying back home, especially for children. *Pasalubong* is often connected with *balikbayan boxes* that are sent home by overseas Filipino workers.

Gurbet From Turkish for "foreign land." *Gurbet* not only designates a geographical location but also implies the emotional distance from home. Stemming from the Arabic *garb*, it means "west" as well as "sunset." The verb garaba also has its root in the same word, meaning "to be removed; to be an alien." The Greek word ξενιτιά (Xenitiá) has a similar meaning.

Heim The term is often used by the German-Turkish community as an abbreviation for the dormitories for so-called guest workers. Migrant workers from Turkey and other countries travelling to Germany with work contracts initially had to live in dormitories, where they shared bedrooms, cooked in communal kitchens, and sometimes even slept in alternating shifts. These dormitories were mostly located directly on the factory premises.

Jus Sanguinis (Latin, right of blood) Under *Jus Sanguinis*, a child is granted citizenship only if at least one parent is a citizen of the State.

Jus Soli (Latin, lit. right of the soil) Under *Jus Soli*, a country confers citizenship on all children born on the territory of the State, irrespective of their parents' nationality.

Kofferkinder Literally from the German "suitcase children," the term was employed for the first time in 1986 by Maria Papoulias. She describes children who, due to labor migration, are left behind by their parents, and in some cases later rejoin them in Germany. Widely applied to labor migration to Germany in the 1960s and 1970s, the term succinctly expresses the "constant sitting on packed suitcases." Many 'suitcase children' also had to repeatedly commute back and forth between their country of origin and Germany.

Laleli A neighbourhood in Istanbul's old city widely known for its dense migrant population. In the 1990s, *Laleli* was the hub for "suitcase trading," the unregistered and duty-free trade of goods, mostly operated by traders from Russia and countries in the former Soviet Union. Many shops in Laleli to this day exclusively sell textiles to Russia and its satellite nations. Numerous forwarding companies have thus established themselves in the district. Many Central Asian migrants spend their free time there, sending parcels to their families back home, eating specialties from their native lands, or visiting the hairdresser.

Pendelkinder See **Kofferkinder**

Remittances The term *remittances* designates money transfers made by migrants to their countries of origin. For some countries, remittances represent a huge economic asset.

Rotation Principle When the first 'guest workers' came to Germany, they were initially issued work and residence permit for one year only. The rationale behind this principle was that after this period, the workers would return to their countries of origin and be replaced by newcomers.

Return Premium In 1983, a return premium was initiated in Germany, whereby unemployed guest workers would receive a payment of DM 10,500, plus DM 1,500 per child, in the event of a definitive departure with the entire family to their country of origin.

Transnationalism The concept was mainly shaped in the 1990s as an opposition to theories of assimilation and integration. *Transnationalism* describes the process of migrants holding social and emotional connections and linking social fields from their country of origin and their country of settlement.

Transmigrants See **Transnationalism**: migrants who are socially connected to their countries of origin as well as their country of settlement.

Transnational Mothers Or **transnational mothering**: With ever more migrants employed in the care sector, more and more women are working abroad to provide for their families. *Transnational mothers* are those women who work abroad and leave one or more children in the care of relatives, friends, or paid nurses.

Western Union The American financial and cash transfer service is used by migrant workers worldwide to transfer money to their home countries.

ξενιτιά (Xenitiá) Greek term for the foreign lands in context of migration, but also the emotional state created by somebody being abroad. See also: **Gurbet**

Yatılı hizmetli Turkish for live-in domestic workers. Current upper class building complexes and gated communities often have an extra room especially for these full-time employees. At the same time there has been a tradition of live-in domestic workers in Turkey, for since the 1950s it was commonplace to employ young women from rural villages, offering them education in exchange for domestic help.

Заробітчанки (zarobitchanka) Ukrainian for wage-earner. The term denotes a female labour migrant who through the force of circumstances has to go abroad in search of work, leaving her family and children behind, in order to earn money for the family upkeep.

Timeline

1930

14 June 1934

The 1934 Resettlement Law was adopted by the Turkish government to oversee the immigration of migrants (so-called national refugees) of "Turkish culture or origin" to Turkey.

1940

23 May 1949

Foundation of the Federal Republic of Germany and the signing of the *Grundgesetz* (Basic Constitutional Law. Article 6 of the *Grundgesetz* reads: (1) Marriage and family shall enjoy the special protection of the State. (2) The care and upbringing of children is the natural right of parents and a duty primarily incumbent upon them. The State shall watch over them in the performance of this duty.

1950

10 November 1954

Headline in the Hamburg daily *Echo*: "Foreign workers instead of Recruits." The Federal Minister of Economic Affairs was negotiating with the Italian Foreign Minister for work permits for Italian migrant workers in the agricultural sector.

20 December 1955

The Federal Republic of Germany concluded a recruitment agreement with Italy. It regulated the recruitment of workers from Italy, as well as selection criteria for applicants. Family reunification could be requested if applicants could demonstrate that adequate living space was available.

1960

29 March 1960

Recruitment agreement between the Federal Republic of Germany and Greece. An estimated one million Greeks worked at least temporarily in Germany over the course of this recruitment agreement, a figure that corresponded to one-tenth of the Greek population at that time.

30 October 1961

Recruitment agreement between the Federal Republic of Germany and Turkey. The recruitment agreement with Turkey initially stated that only unmarried persons could be recruited, and that family reunification or family reunion was excluded. The length of stay in Germany was restricted to two years.

November 1961

The first special train, known as the *kara tren* [black train], for Turkish guest workers operated between Istanbul Sirkeci station and Munich.

10 December 1961

Upon arriving at the station Cologne-Deutz, Armando Rodrigues de Sá from Portugal was declared to be the millionth guest worker to enter Germany. He was presented with a Zündapp moped and a bouquet of flowers.

19 May 1964

In an amended version of 1961 the agreement with Turkey, the Rotation Principle was repealed and the prohibition of family reunification by migrant workers from Turkey was abolished.

1965

The Foreigners Act was initially introduced. This law defined different types of residence permits for those entering Germany: A newly-arrived foreigner would receive a residence permit, as would family members who subsequently come to Germany. A right of residence permit was only granted after a foreigner had lived in the Federal Republic for at least eight years.

1965

Germany: The Federal government introduced mandatory education for non-German children. This regulation impacted the final decision by many migrant parents about whether to bring their children to Germany, or to leave them in their home country, thereby making it more difficult to send them back and forth.

12 October 1968

Recruitment agreement between the Federal Republic of Germany and the Socialist Federal Republic of Yugoslavia. It was in this context that the term *Gastarbeiter* [guest worker] was first mentioned. Reunification or family reunion was excluded. The length of stay in Germany was restricted to two years.

1969

Maiden direct flight between Hamburg and Turkey. Vural Öger established the travel agency Reisebüro Istanbul, from which emerged Öger Türk Tours GmbH in 1973.

1970

12 March 1971

Military coup in Turkey. Suleiman Demirel's government was accused of being responsible for the country's social and economic grievances following fierce political turmoil, mass demonstrations and numerous workers' strikes. Demirel and his government resigned after receiving a Memorandum from the military generals.

23 November 1973

The Federal Government in Germany instigated a recruitment ban that impacted all countries with which a recruitment agreement had been concluded. For those migrant workers already living in the Federal Republic, the recruitment stop had no consequences. Legally regulated family reunification allowed them to bring their relatives to Germany under certain conditions.

1974

Philippines: A "contract labor" system was initiated in reaction to financial vulnerabilities caused by the 1973 Oil Crisis. Since launching the system the government excelled in locating emerging or expanding markets in need of foreign labour and in making bilateral agreements with the related governments to provide the required labour force.

30 November 1974

The Federal Government of Germany issued a "cut-off date" regulation: All family members moving to Germany after the 30.11.1974 – including adolescents – would no longer receive a work permit. However, a short time later, the deadline for applying for a work permit for adolescent migrants was delayed until 31 December 1976.

1975

As of January 1975, child benefit payments for migrant worker's children not living in Germany was considerably modified. While those children living in the country of origin would continue to receive child benefits they had hitherto received, the increased amount was henceforth only paid to children living with their parents in Germany. This change in the child benefit regime was a crucial factor behind many children being brought to Germany by their parents.

1979

In the Kühn Memorandum – named after the Commissioner for Foreigners Heinz Kühn – Germany was for the first time publicly referred to as a land of immigration. The Memorandum also stated that "guest workers" must be afforded the possibility of lasting integration. It also envisaged unlimited education and work permits for foreign youths, the right to naturalization for adolescents born or raised in Germany from immigrant families, as well as full legal equality for foreigners living in Germany.

1 April 1979

Repeal of regulations for access to German labour market (cut-off dates). Henceforth access to employment by family members of foreign workers was contingent upon waiting time regulations. Spouses of guest workers in Germany, irrespective of their date of entry into Germany, were entitled to a work permit after a four-year waiting period. Adolescents were entitled to receive a work permit or a training place after a two-year waiting period.

1980

12 September 1975

Military coup in Turkey. General Kenan Evren declared live on TRT, Turkish State Television, that he had taken power.

8 December 1981

Resolutions by the German Federal Government and the individual Federal States restricting family reunification: Children over the age of sixteen were henceforth not allowed to enter the Federal Republic of Germany to rejoin their parents. If one parent lived in the country of origin, younger children were also not allowed to enter Germany. Spouses from Turkey could only reunify with German citizens who had legally lived in the Federal Republic for at least eight years without interruption; the waiting period was one to three years.

13 December 1983

Turgut Özal, 45th President of Republic of Turkey, began his term of office. During his presidency, a structural change program based on free market regulations came into force. Turkey opened up its markets for imports and exports.

28 November 1983

The Return Assistance Act meant to encourage the repatriation of foreign nationals living in Germany by means of return premiums came into force. In the event of a definitive departure, whereby the entire migrant family departed Germany, a return premium of 10,500DM, in addition to 1,500DM per child, was paid.

30 June 1987

In recognition of sending remittances that contributed toward national recovery efforts, Philippine President Corazon Aquino enacted a law providing duty- and tax-free status to so-called *balik-bayan* boxes, which contained presents and goods sent to the Philippines by overseas Filipino workers (OFWs).

25 December 1989

The Romanian dictator Nicolae Ceausescu and his wife Elena Ceausescu were executed by a group of elite soldiers after being charged, inter alia, with subversion of state power and genocide. After the fall of the communist regime Romania opened up to the West.

1990

2 August 1990

Turkey became a major destination among Filipino migration networks in the early 1990s due to its pivotal location between Europe and the Middle East. Turkey emerged as a transit location for those wishing to pursue employment opportunities elsewhere. Some found works and settled in Turkey while waiting to move on to Europe. During this period Turkey became a plausible option for those seeking employment.

26 April 1990

Amended version of the 1965 Foreigners Act was implemented. *Jus Sanguinis* (right of descent) remained in force. Only persons of German descent were recognized as German citizens. Children of migrants born in the Federal Republic of Germany were not granted German citizenship even if the family had already lived in Germany for two generations.

1990s Suitcase Trade

The suitcase trade, mainly operated by women from the former Asian Soviet republics refers to Turkish exports to Russia and its satellite nations, with returning passengers packing their luggage with merchandise to sell outside Turkey. The liberalization of the Turkish trade regime in the 1980s and the collapse of the Soviet Union in 1991 provided fertile ground for the emergence of the suitcase trade. The trading women started regularly traveling between countries and many of them later continued working in Turkey as domestic workers.

3 October 1990

German Reunification

1990

With the arrival of the Filipinos who had fled nations engulfed in the Gulf War, followed in 1989 by Bulgarians, and later by Moldovans economically affected by the 1998 Russian banking crisis, an increase in full-employment of domestic workers could be observed in Turkey. Known as bakıcı [caregiver] or yatılı hizmetli [live-in domestic], these workers lived full-time with their employers.

25 December 1991

Collapse and dissolution of the Soviet Union. While better known as a migrant "sender" nation, Turkey was to become a host nation for migrants from the former Soviet Union and the socialist sphere; this was mostly due to the ease and low cost of illegal entry and finding illegal work, but also because of language skills in the case of Turcic people such as the Gagauz.

7 February 1992

The Maastricht Treaty introduced the idea of citizenship of the Union. It did not replace citizenship of the individual EU states, but rather complemented them. EU citizenship was granted to anyone holding citizenship of one of the member states of the EU. An EU citizen was, inter alia, thus entitled to obtain a residence permit throughout the Union.

30 June 1993

An amendment to the 1965 Foreigners Act entitled foreign nationals born in Germany, or those who had lived there for more than fifteen years, to a legal right to demand naturalization.

1997/1998

Introduction of visa requirement for children under sixteen from counties of ex-Yugoslavia and from Morocco. Hitherto, parents could at will register and deregister their own children, as well as those of relatives in Germany.

2000

In Germany, *Jus Sanguinis* (right of descent) was supplemented by elements of the so-called birthplace principle. Thereafter, persons born in Germany and having a parent who had lived more than eight years in Germany with a lawful residence permit, was also deemed German.

2001

The 2001 economic crisis caused a significant decrease in demand for migrant domestic workers in Turkey. After the impact of the crisis had alleviated, a fresh wave of domestic migrant workers started coming from Georgia, Azerbaijan, Armenia, Turkmenistan, and Uzbekistan. To employ a migrant domestic worker became a characteristic of the Turkish middle classes.

27 February 2003

Law on Work Permits of Foreigners in Turkey: The Ministry of Labor and Social Security (MoLSS) granted permission to employ foreigners, considering the needs of the domestic labour market and under the condition that no domestic laborers could be found for the job position.

29 August 2003

The first public beta version of Skype was launched. Video communication programs opened up a new era for transnational families and inter-family relationships.

1 January 2007

Romania and Bulgaria joined the EU as the 26th and 27th member States. Despite the law on the free movement of workers across the EU, Germany initially denied citizens of these two member states access to its labour market. The labour market in Germany has only been fully open as of 1 January 2014 for job-seekers from Romania and Bulgaria.

7 April 2009

Judgment by the Federal Administrative Court: When establishing whether it could be expected that the means of subsistence for a child resident in the Federal territory of Germany could be secured by dint of its parents' income and without recourse to public funds, the parents' statutory maintenance obligations for other children have to be taken into accounted. Hence, the bigger the family, the more difficult it was for children to be reunited with their parents.

2010

1 February 2012

Amendment to Law on Foreigners' Residence and Travel in Turkey: Tourist visas were henceforth no longer valid for a maximum of 90 days, but rather for 90 days within a 180-day period. Previously, it was possible for migrants to leave Turkey before their visa expired and directly return with a new tourist visa. Following the introduction of the new law, migrant domestic workers now have the option to either work illegally after their visa expires, or to find an employer willing to apply for a work permit on their behalf, but then find themselves forced to remain with that employer.

18 March 2016

Refugee agreement between the EU and Turkey: Asylum seekers, who use Turkey as a transit country and enter the territory of the EU for the first time via the Greek islands, are to be deported back to Turkey. For each Syrian citizen deported from the Greek islands to Turkey, another Syrian citizen in Turkey is to be resettled in the EU (1:1 mechanism). In return, Turkey's EU accession negotiations were to be accelerated, and a visa waiver for Turkish citizens was to be introduced as of October 2016. To date, these have not materialized.

2017

Draft legislation in Germany concerning child benefit payments. Henceforth payments should be adjusted to the cost of living of the state in which the child is resident. These child benefit regulations apply to children entitled to child benefit payments in Germany, but whose place of residence is another EU member State.

June 2017

Introduction of a visa-free regime for Ukrainian citizens traveling to and across the EU for up to 90 days. This does not entitle them to a work permit. Many migrants employed in the cleaning and care sectors avail of this opportunity and commute back and forth to Ukraine.

2016-2018

Suspension of family reunification for subsidiary protection in Germany. According to the current regulation, family members, who are entitled to subsidiary protection and whose residence permit was issued after 17 March 2016, are not eligible to apply for family reunification under the Residence Act until 31 July 2018.

1 February 2018

Draft legislation for Family Reunification of Subsidiary Beneficiaries. As of 1 August 2018, one-thousand spouses and minors or parents of subsidiary protected minors shall be granted asylum per month. Hardship provisions are not included in this legislation. Implementation details are still unclear. Eva Högl, vice-chairperson of the Socialist parliamentary group in the Bundestag, referred to dealing with those seeking protection as an "indicator of how seriously we are about human dignity and protecting the family."

Text Credits

78 Corobca, L. 2015. *Der erste Horizont meines Lebens.* [My life's first Horizon] Vienna: Paul Zsolnay. Translated into English by Bogdan Lepadatu.

84 Kruk, H. 2013. Ho Paura. In: Brunner, K., Sawka, M. & Onufriv, S. (ed.) *Skype Mama.* Berlin: edition.foto TAPETA.

54 Matzouranis, G. 1985. *Man nennt uns Gastarbeiter.* [They call us Gastarbeiter.] Frankfurt am Main: Zambon.

50 Papoulias, M. 1987. Die "Kofferkinder". Mutter-Kind Trennung als Ursache für psychopathologische Reaktionen bei Familien von Arbeitsmigranten. [Suitcase Children. Mother-Child Separation as a Cause of Psychopathological Reactions among Migrant Worker Families.] In: Morten, A.1987. (ed.) *Hören Sie Stimmen?" Beiträge zur Migrationspsychiatrie im Rahmen der 38. Gütersloher Fortbildungswoche 1986* ["Do you hear voices?" Contributions to Migration Psychiatry in the framework of the 38th Gütersloh Training Week 1986.] pp. 49-52. Gütersloh: Jakob van Hoddis.

64 Polis, Stefano. 2011. *Milch in Papier. Kindheit und Jugend zwischen zwei Kulturen. Autobiographische Erzählungen.* [Milk in Paper. Childhood and Adolescence between two Cultures. Autobiographical Stories.] Frankfurt am Main: Grössenwahn.

38 Wilhelm, Gülcin. 2011. *Generation Koffer: Die zurückgelassenen Kinder.* [Generation Suitcase: The Children Left Behind] Berlin: Orlanda.

Image Credits

PP. 47-48: Ok-Hee Jeong
PP. 60-61: Historisch Beeldarchief Migranten [Historical Image Archive of Migrants Amsterdam]
PP. 62-63: DOMiD-Archiv Köln
PP. 15-16: private
PP. 83: private
PP. 91-92: private
PP. 126-127: private
PP. 152-169: Felix Kayser

Songs and Video Credits

94 Nebahat Yıldız, *Babamızı gönder Almanya.* 197?. Istanbul: Sevilen.

96 Meho Puzić, *Meho Puzić - Moj brate u tudjini - (Audio)*, YouTube video, 3:51, October 29, 2015, https://www.youtube.com/watch?v=jZ1cMf1-tEc.

98 Stelios Kazantzidis, *ΤΟ ΨΩΜΙ ΤΗΣ ΞΕΝΗΤΙΑΣ - ΣΤΕΛΙΟΣ ΚΑΖΑΝΤΖΙΔΗΣ*, YouTube video, 3:21, April 26, 2017, https://www.youtube.com/watch?v=ICi8s-RyBnMk.

100 Mickey Bustos, *Balikbayan Box (Pinoy Wrecking Ball Parody)*, YouTube video, 4:12, December 11, 2013, https://www.youtube.com/watch?v=WSMw7trHUcU&index=26&list=PLg_aTjVGL1EP0McWqc-8NQFT1Kajwsvn6j.

104 Antonia Stoian, *Antonia Stoian Ai plecat mama departe*, YouTube video, 4:35, December 23, 2011, https://www.youtube.com/watch?v=GpYDTQDqkgl.

108 Unknown, *O strofa pentru copii care au parintii la munca in strainatate*, YouTube video 0:59, February 2, 2016, https://www.youtube.com/watch?v=tsYXcCWB-JSo&index-=3&list=PLg_aTjVGL1EP0M-cWqc8NQFT1Kajwsvn6j.

112 Denisa, *Denisa - Sterge mama lacrima*, YouTube video, 4:09, January 10, 2011, https://www.youtube.com/watch?v=b_Bx-nvNAt0E.

116 Violetta Timofieva, *Віолетта Тимофієва "Мати-емігрантка" автор пісні Ірина Лончина*, YouTube video, 5:13, September 18, 2014, https://www.youtube.com/watch?v=dNNLjp9iVqc&feature=youtu.be

122 Vasyl Danyliuk, *Василь Данилюк - Заробітчанки*, 2007, YouTube video, 4:30, June 21, 2012, https://www.youtube.com/watch?v=GjwbGsTzjV4&feature=youtu.be

Publishers

bi'bak (Turkish: have a look) is a non-profit organization based in Berlin, where it runs a project space. Engaged in transnational narratives, migration, and global mobility bi'bak puts a focus on the aesthetic dimensions. bi'bak's program examines diverse disciplines in art, science, and community development, including film screenings, exhibitions, workshops as well as music events and culinary excursions. bi'bak believes in a decentralised and rhizomatic connection between art, design, sciences, participation, urban/ public space, and local activism.

Archive is a platform for cultural research and debate. It brings together activists and cultural practitioners in an adaptable structure that aims to foster a unique space for discussion and exchange. Archive is engaged in a wide range of activities including publishing and exhibition making. *Archive Books* produces monographs, readers' and artists' books, as well as journals focusing on contemporary cultural production and reception. Located in Berlin, *Archive Kabinett* is both a library/bookshop showcasing a selected range of printed matters, and simultaneously a space for lectures, screenings, and exhibitions. *Archive Journal* is a cross-disciplinary journal primarily concerned with the notion of documentation but also with contemporary uses of translation and circulation. *Archive Appendix* is the design department that brings a conceptual approach to the relation between text and image.

Collaborative Partners

DEPO is a space for culture, arts and critical debate in Istanbul. DEPO focuses on practices dealing with historical and contemporary social issues. Its program includes exhibitions, screenings, panel discussions, workshops, and presentations and it publishes an online journal *Red Thread*. DEPO aims at becoming a hub where politically and socially engaged projects can be realized, and to provide artists, curators, cultural operators, academics, researchers, and a wide audience with a platform for exchange of ideas and experiences. DEPO is an initiative by Anadolu Kültür (www.anadolukultur.org), a not-for-profit organization working in the field of culture. Through various projects, Anadolu Kültür strives to support local regional initiatives, to emphasize cultural diversity and cultural rights, and to strengthen interregional and international collaboration.

DOMiD – Documentation Centre and Museum of Migration in Germany

Located in Cologne, DOMiD was founded in 1990 by migrants so as to preserve immigrants' historical heritage. Today, DOMiD is home to a unique nationwide collection of over 150,000 social, everyday, and cultural historical testimonies on the history of immigration to Germany. It considers its task to research and exhibit this collection. It is thus one of the key players in the field of the culture of remembrance in the migration society. In addition to its museum and archival work, DOMiD organizes events, conferences, and lectures on related topics. Currently, DOMiD is working toward realizing a central Migration Museum in Germany and is about to open a virtual Migration Museum.

Artistic Directors

Malve Lippmann studied at the State Academy of Fine Arts Stuttgart and at the Institute for Art in Context at the Berlin University of the Arts (MA). She worked as a freelance stage and costume designer in the field of opera, performance, and theatrical productions. Malve was in charge of the design of various performance, art, and theatre projects in other European countries, Russia, and the USA. She is co-founder and artistic director of bi'bak, based in Berlin.

Can Sungu studied film and visual communication design in Istanbul and at the Institute for Art in Context at the Berlin University of the Arts. He has given workshops and seminars in the field of film and published texts on film and migration. As an artist, he participated in numerous exhibitions, including at MMSU Rijeka, Künstlerhaus Vienna, DEPO

Istanbul and REDCAT Los Angeles. He is co-founder and artistic director of the project space bi'bak in Berlin.

Editor

Maike Suhr studied social and business communication (MA) at the Berlin University of the Arts. She conducts research on transnationalism and material culture. She is currently working as a freelance editor.

Authors

Ayşe Akalın studied sociology, political science and international relations in Istanbul and New York. Her PhD examines foreign domestic workers in Turkey. She teaches at Istanbul Technical University, where her focus is on gender and migration.

Liliana Corobca, born in Saseni-Calarasi in Moldova, is a literary scholar and writer living in Bucharest. She has published six novels, a play, and several books on censorship of literature in communist Romania. Her novel *Kinderland* was published in the autumn of 2013.

Ok-Hee Jeong was born in South Korea and came to Germany when she was eight years old. She studied arts and Korean studies and currently works as a free journalist, filmmaker, and author in Berlin.

Halyna Kruk is a poet, translator, and children's book writer based in Lviv. She has authored five poetry collections, the latest in 2017 under the title *An Adult Women*. Kruk is a vice-president of the Ukrainian PEN International and a professor of literary studies at Lviv National University.

Georg Matzouranis is a writer and journalist. Born in Athens, he studied political sciences in Athens and journalistic studies in Munich, where he lived from 1966 to 1976. *Man nennt uns Gastarbeiter* [They Call Us Gastarbeiter] counts as a pioneering work on Greek 'guest workers' and immigration.

Maria Papoulias is a psychologist. In 1987, she published the article *The Suitcase Children – Mother-Child Separation as the Cause of Psychopathological Reactions among Families of Migrant Workers* in an anthology of the now defunct Jakob van Hoddis' publishing house, thereby coining the term 'suitcase children'.

Stefano Polis born in 1965 in Kozani, Greece, spent his childhood and adolescent years as a so-called suitcase child commuting between Greece and Germany, where his parents were working. Polis currently runs a hairdresser's salon in Jülich near Düren. *Milk in Paper* is his first novel.

Janka Vogel, born in 1988, is a social worker and a researcher in Romanian studies. She writes and researches on topics such as South-eastern Europe, Romanian migration and diaspora, as well as European and socio-political issues. She is currently working as a social worker with Romanian migrants in Berlin.

Gülcin Wilhelm, born in Istanbul, lives in Berlin since 1977. She worked for the weekly *Der Freitag* for many years in various capacities. She currently works as a freelance publicist and translator.

Published by:

bi'bak, www.bi-bak.de

Archive Books, www.archive-books.org

On the occasion of the exhibition

Bitter Things – Narratives and Memories
of Transnational Families

Istanbul, Depo:
18 May – 24 June 2018

Berlin, Archive Kabinett:
14 September – 12 Oktober 2018

Concept and Artistic Direction:

Malve Lippmann, Can Sungu

Editing, Research:

Maike Suhr

Translations:

John Barrett, Aaron Lajos Cotaru,
Ian Clotworthy, Bogdan Lepadatu,
Ivanna Zakharevych

Proofreading:

Daisy Nutting

Archive DOMID:

Bettina Just, Beate Rieple,
Bengü Kocatürk-Schuster

Project Assistants:

Zeynep Dişbudak, Esra Akkaya

Graphic Design:

Archive Appendix

Printer:

BUD Potsdam

Printrun:

600

Contributing Authors:

Ayşe Akalın

Liliana Corobca

Ok-Hee Jeong

Halyna Kruk

Georg Matzouranis

Maria Papoulias

Stefano Polis

Janka Vogel

Gülcin Wilhelm

With Thanks to:

Lena Alpozan, Duygu Atçeken, Duru Bekler, Aslı
Çetinkaya, Gabi Cotaru, Johann Cotaru, Michel Bourse,
Alin Deju, Vanessa Deju, Semra Deniz, Eleftheria
Gavriilidou, Rozahal Gayıpova, Yuriy Gurzhy, Asena Günal,
Adela Hader, Ok-Hee Jeong, Nikolay Karabinovych,
Bengü Kocatürk-Schuster, Eleftheria Koukoura, Tülin Melillo,
Olga Mishkina, Gülşah Mursaoğlu, Ayşenur Müslümanoğlu,
Rosie Müller, Persefoni Myrtsou, Selim Özadar, Andreas
Rostek, Vanessa Sabelski, Sewastos Sampsounis,
Emre Senan, Florin Ştefan, Nataša Šuković, Alev Sungu,
Anita Surkić, Angelos Tsaousis, Dimitrios Zachos

and to all our interviewees, who deliberately wish to
remain anonymous.

ISBN 978-3-943620-79-5
Printed in Germany,
All rights reserved
© Berlin, 2018

A project by: 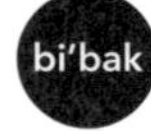

in collaboration with:

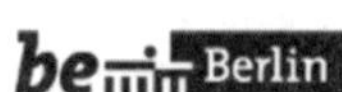

With the support of:

The Berlin Senate Department
for Culture and Europe